Getting to Work on **Summer Learning**

Recommended Practices for Success

Catherine H. Augustine, Jennifer Sloan McCombs,
Heather L. Schwartz, Laura Zakaras

Commissioned by

The Wallace Foundation

Supporting ideas.
Sharing solutions.
Expanding opportunities.

RAND
CORPORATION

The research in this report was produced within RAND Education, a unit of the RAND Corporation. The research was commissioned by The Wallace Foundation.

Library of Congress Cataloging-in-Publication Data

The RAND Corporation is a nonprofit institution that helps improve policy and decisionmaking through research and analysis. RAND's publications do not necessarily reflect the opinions of its research clients and sponsors.

Support RAND—make a tax-deductible charitable contribution at www.rand.org/giving/contribute.html

RAND® is a registered trademark.

Cover design by Dori Gordon Walker

© Copyright 2013 RAND Corporation

RAND OFFICES
SANTA MONICA, CA • WASHINGTON, DC
PITTSBURGH, PA • NEW ORLEANS, LA • JACKSON, MS • BOSTON, MA
DOHA, QA • CAMBRIDGE, UK • BRUSSELS, BE
www.rand.org

Preface

This report offers guidance to district leaders across the country who are interested in launching summer learning programs or improving programs that are already established. Our recommendations are based on the evaluations of summer programs in six urban districts in the summer of 2011. These districts—Boston; Cincinnati; Dallas; Duval County, Florida; Pittsburgh; and Rochester, New York—were selected for a multiyear demonstration project funded by The Wallace Foundation to assess their effectiveness in improving student achievement. They are among the nation's most advanced in their experience with comprehensive, voluntary summer learning programs.

This is the second of five reports that will result from the evaluation. The first report, *Making Summer Count: How Summer Programs Can Boost Children's Learning* (McCombs et al., 2011) synthesized the research on summer learning loss, identified the key features of effective summer learning programs supported by research, and investigated the ways that more than 20 program leaders were managing the challenges of implementing such programs. This second report offers lessons learned from detailed evaluations of the district programs in the demonstration project in the summer of 2011. These evaluations were designed to help the districts improve the programs they offered in 2012. We have since completed evaluations of the summer 2012 programs, so that districts could further strengthen their programs by the summer of 2013, during a randomized controlled trial to assess the programs' effects on student performance. Three forthcoming reports will present the results of the trial. A PDF file containing the appendix material to this document is available on the RAND website's product page for this research report (http://www.rand.org/pubs/research_reports/RR366.html).

This study was undertaken by RAND Education, a unit of the RAND Corporation that conducts research on prekindergarten, kindergarten–12th grade, and higher education issues such as assessment and accountability, choice-based and standards-based school reform, vocational training, and the value of arts education and policy in sustaining and promoting well-rounded communities.

This study was sponsored by The Wallace Foundation, which seeks to support and share effective ideas and practices to improve learning and enrichment opportunities for children. Its current objectives are to improve the quality of schools, primarily by developing and placing effective principals in high-need schools; improving the quality of and access to after-school programs through coordinated city systems and by strengthening the financial management skills of providers; reimagining and expanding learning time during the traditional school day and year as well as during the summer months; expanding access to arts learning; and developing audiences for the arts. For more information and research on these and other related topics, please visit its Knowledge Center at www.wallacefoundation.org.

Contents

CHAPTER FOUR

Teacher Selection and Training

CHAPTER FIVE

Enrichment Activities

CHAPTER SIX

Attendance

Figures and Tables

Figures

Tables

Summary

Summer learning programs have emerged as a promising way to address the growing achievement gap between children of the poorest families and those of the most affluent. Research shows that during summer, low-income students suffer disproportionate learning loss and those losses accumulate over time, contributing substantially to the achievement gap between low- and higher-income children. In addition, summer programs can benefit struggling students of all backgrounds by providing additional time to learn material they did not master during the school year. Many school districts offer mandatory summer programs to students at risk of grade retention, but fewer districts offer summer learning programs to a broader population of students as a means of stemming summer learning loss and boosting academic performance.

The Wallace Foundation is funding a multiyear demonstration project to determine whether district summer learning programs can stem summer learning loss for low-income students. This report distills the lessons learned so far from evaluations of programs offered in summer 2011 in six districts selected for the demonstration project. These districts—Boston; Cincinnati; Dallas; Duval County, Florida; Pittsburgh; and Rochester, New York—have committed to offering such programs to large numbers of at-risk elementary students. These are all voluntary programs that offer reading, mathematics, and enrichment activities (such as arts, sports, and science exploration); operate for a full day; provide transportation to students; are free of charge; and share a goal of maintaining or improving student achievement. They all served students rising from third into fourth grade (the focus of our evaluations), and most districts served other grade levels as well.

To gather information for our evaluations, we interviewed summer program stakeholders, such as district leaders and summer site leaders and teachers; surveyed teachers, parents, and students; observed program training, instruction, and logistics; engaged professors of elementary education reading and mathematics to review the curricula; gathered program cost data; and analyzed district data on attendance. Our analysis of all this information, combined with our review of education research (including studies of the characteristics of strong summer programs), led to a diagnosis of the key strengths and weaknesses of each program, as well as recommendations for improvement tailored to each district. The detailed evaluations that went to each district were designed to help them improve their programs before the summer of 2013, when we will conduct a randomized controlled trial to answer the key question: Are these programs improving student outcomes?

Although the demonstration project is not yet complete, we synthesized the key lessons we have learned so far and developed a set of recommendations. Because there is demand for information on how to set up and manage such programs, we did not want to wait until the end of the study to share what we have learned about what works and what does not. Although the recommendations we make here are not proven practices—we do not yet have student outcome data from the randomized controlled trial—they are based on an enormous data-gathering effort that included more than 1,800 surveys, 325 interviews, and about 400 hours of direct observations of classroom and enrichment activities. We are confident that these recommendations offer the best guidance on summer programs currently available.

In the accompanying box we list these recommendations, organized around the key challenges of starting up and managing a summer learning program.

Recommendations

Planning

Launching a summer program is akin to starting a new school year, but with less time for planning and execution. A good planning process may be the most important characteristic of a strong program: It reduces logistical problems and increases instructional time for students.

1. **Start early and be inclusive.**
   - Commit to having a summer program by January.
   - Include both district and site-level staff in the planning process.
   - Centralize some decisionmaking.
   - Deliver planning templates to site leaders.
2. **Meet regularly and be comprehensive in scope.**
   - Conduct regular and productive meetings before the program starts.
   - Plan for enrichment activities as well as academics.
3. **Clearly delineate roles.**
   - Among program leaders, external partners, and summer site leaders, determine who will plan for what and who will be responsible for what during the summer.
4. **Establish firm enrollment deadlines and keep electronic student records.**

Curriculum and Instruction

Summer programs are short and often provide little time for teachers to plan their lessons. To maximize the effectiveness of instruction, teachers must have high-quality curricular materials, matched to student needs and small class sizes. These strategies, which characterized the best curriculum and instruction across districts, are likely to lead to stronger student outcomes.

1. **Anchor the program in a commercially available and evidence-based curriculum.**

2. **Standardize the curriculum across district sites.**

3. **Include strategies for differentiation in curriculum materials to accommodate at least two ability levels.**

4. **Structure the program to ensure sufficient time on task.**

5. **Instruct students in small classes or groups.**

6. **Provide support to students with special needs.**

Teacher Selection and Training

According to the research, teaching quality has the largest school-based impact on student outcomes of any factor. Hiring effective teachers and giving them the support they need are critical steps to maximizing student achievement.

1. Recruit and hire the right teachers.
  – Develop rigorous selection processes to recruit motivated teachers.
  – Take teachers' school-year performance into consideration.
  – Hire teachers with grade-level and subject-matter experience and, if possible, familiarity with the students.
  – Negotiate with teachers' unions, if necessary, to establish a competitive selection process.

2. Give teachers sufficient training and ongoing support.
  – Familiarize teachers with the summer curriculum and how to teach it.
  – Help teachers tailor the curriculum for students with different aptitudes.
  – Provide ongoing support to implement the curriculum.
  – Include all instructional support staff in academic training sessions.
  – Give teachers time to set up their classrooms in advance.

Enrichment Activities

All districts included fun and engaging enrichment activities such as the arts, sports, and science exploration to differentiate their programs from traditional summer school and to attract students and promote attendance. Some good practices characterized the most well-organized and engaging activities we observed in the districts.

1. Keep class sizes small and select providers with well-qualified staff who have experience in behavior management.

2. Conduct careful planning if enrichment is supposed to be integrated with academics.

Attendance

Research has confirmed the common-sense notion that in order for students to benefit from summer programs, they must attend regularly. In addition to offering enrichment activities, some districts adopted other effective strategies for maintaining good attendance.

1. **Set enrollment deadlines.**
2. **Establish a clear attendance policy.**
3. **Provide field trips and other incentives for students who attend.**
4. **Keep in mind it is not necessary to disguise academics to boost attendance.**

Time on Task

The ultimate goal of summer learning programs is to improve academic achievement. Besides providing high-quality instruction and achieving good attendance, a program needs to be structured to provide a sufficient amount of time on academics to improve performance.

1. **Operate the program for five to six weeks.**
2. **Schedule three to four hours a day for academics and focus on academic content during those hours.**

Program Cost and Funding

Cost is a key barrier in creating and sustaining summer learning programs. However, districts can better estimate and minimize costs—as well as maximizing value from an investment in summer learning—by following these recommendations.

1. **Design the summer program with costs in mind.**
   - To control fixed costs, avoid assigning small numbers of students to many sites.
   - Use enrichment providers to help leverage additional funds and provide a full-day program.
   - Hire staff to achieve desired student-to-adult ratios based on projected daily attendance, not the initial number of enrollees.
   - Operate full-day programs for five to six weeks.
2. **Put resources into tracking and boosting attendance.**
3. **Use effective cost-accounting practices.**
   - To understand costs per student served, express costs on not just a per-enrollee basis, but also on a per-attendee, per-hour basis.
   - Set up data procedures to enable cost tracking on a per-attendee, per-hour basis.

Acknowledgments

Many people helped in conducting this study and producing this report. We would like to thank those at The Wallace Foundation for their substantive and financial support. In particular, Edward Pauly and Ann Stone provided valuable guidance on the intellectual and analytic components of our work. Pam Mendels and Lucas Held provided greatly appreciated feedback on this report.

Representatives from the Boston, Cincinnati, Dallas, Duval County, Pittsburgh, and Rochester summer programs generously allowed us access to their programs for observation and time to interview and survey stakeholders. We are particularly grateful to the people who allowed us to interview them and to those who completed the surveys. Although we are keeping their identities confidential, their insights, opinions, and ideas greatly contributed to this report. Program materials and district data were provided when requested and we appreciate the time that went into fulfilling those requests.

Several RAND staff members contributed to the formative evaluations and therefore to this report. Melissa Bradley coordinated the institutional review board processes within RAND and with each district and coordinated survey administration in the six districts. Alexandria Felton, Courtney Kase, Dahlia Lichter, Terry Marsh, Andrea Phillips, and Lucrecia Santibanez collected data in the six districts. Ann Haas, Anna Saavedra, and Stephanie Williamson coordinated acquisition of district data and conducted analyses of both these data and our survey data.

Internal and external reviewers, including Cathy Stasz, Lynn Karoly, and Mary Barrie, improved the document itself. Finally, we thank Arwen Bicknell for her excellent editing services.

Abbreviations

21CCLC	21st Century Community Learning Center
CBO	community-based organization
ELA	English language arts
IDEA-B	Individuals with Disabilities Education Act, Part B
NAEP	National Assessment of Educational Progress
OST	out-of-school time
PSA	Policy Studies Associates
SIG	School Improvement Grants

CHAPTER ONE

Introduction

Despite concerted efforts to close the large achievement gap between disadvantaged and advantaged students over the past several decades, significant disparities remain. On the National Assessment of Educational Progress (NAEP) in 2011, 50 percent of fourth-grade students eligible for free lunch scored at the "below basic" level in reading (the lowest proficiency level), compared with 18 percent of students who were not eligible for the free or reduced-price lunch programs. Large achievement gaps exist for mathematics as well, with 29 percent of students receiving free lunch performing at the lowest performance level compared with only 8 percent of higher-income peers. These trends hold in the eighth grade as well (U.S. Department of Education, undated). Because an inequitable proportion of low-income students is from minority populations, similar achievement gaps are found between white and black children, white and Hispanic children, and native speakers and English language learners.

In fact, the achievement gap between children from the poorest and most affluent families has increased over decades. Examining the data on children from families in the top 10 percent of income and those in the bottom 10 percent, we found the achievement gap to have grown substantially since the mid-1970s: The gap in achievement for children from families in these income groups now is 30 to 60 percent larger than it was for children born in the 1970s from families with the same differences in income (Reardon, 2011).

Not surprisingly, these income and achievement disparities are also associated with differences in levels of educational attainment. Students from the bottom quartile of the income distribution are more than twice as likely to drop out of high school as students from the top quartile of the distribution (Digest of Education Statistics, 2007). Failing to complete high school has significant ramifications for the individuals themselves and for society because formal schooling is an increasingly important gateway to future employment, earnings, and attendant life chances (Belfield and Levin, 2007). As family income has become more predictive of children's academic achievement, educational attainment and cognitive skills have become more predictive of adults' earnings (Reardon, 2011).

It is against this background that policymakers have been considering interventions that could help close the achievement gap. One approach that appears to show promise is expanding learning time, particularly during the summer months. This is because summer vacation contributes to existing achievement and educational attainment gaps. Over the summer, students typically either slow their learning or lose knowledge and skills. On average, students re-enter school in the fall performing about one month behind where they performed in the previous spring (Cooper et al., 1996). We might be willing to accept this "summer slide" if all students experienced these average losses. However, research shows that low-income students lose more knowledge and skills than their more affluent peers. For example, low-income students lose substantial ground in reading during the summer, while their more affluent peers maintain or even gain. There is also evidence that summer learning loss is cumulative: As years pass, low-income students fall farther behind, contributing substantially to the achievement gap in reading skills by the ninth grade (Alexander, Entwisle, and Olson, 2007).

While many school districts offer mandatory summer programs to students at risk of grade retention, this research shows that many more students, including low-income as well as low-achieving students, can benefit from summer learning programs. This report provides ideas and practices that districts can use to support the development and sustainability of such programs.

Study Background

This study stems from research commissioned by The Wallace Foundation as part of its summer learning initiative, the objective of which is to promote high-quality summer learning programs across the country for low-income and low-achieving students. The Foundation is pursuing three strategies:

- building awareness of the problems of summer learning loss, as well as potential solutions
- funding leading providers of summer learning programs so they can serve more children
- evaluating whether and how voluntary summer learning programs in school districts can stem summer learning loss for low-income students.

As part of the third strategy, The Foundation is supporting a summer learning demonstration. This process began in 2010 when The Foundation asked RAND to synthesize the research on features of effective summer learning programs and to investigate how districts are managing implementation challenges. The report from that study, *Making Summer Count: How Summer Programs Can Boost Children's Learning* (McCombs et al., 2011), formed the basis for the design of the summer demonstration programs for low-achieving students.

For the demonstration itself, The Foundation selected six urban districts that had committed themselves to offering a voluntary summer program to large numbers of struggling elementary students, not just those facing grade retention: Boston; Cincinnati; Dallas; Duval County, Florida; Pittsburgh; and Rochester, New York. As pioneers in this arena, these six districts are understandably encountering many of the challenges documented in the report mentioned above. To help them address these difficulties and strengthen their programs so that they could be tested for their effectiveness, The Foundation asked RAND to conduct formative evaluations of the programs over two summers (2011 and 2012) so that districts could make successive improvements to their programs before 2013, when they would be rigorously evaluated to demonstrate the programs' effects on student performance.

This report offers guidance on how to launch and sustain summer learning programs based on what we learned from the evaluations conducted in the summer of 2011 and our review of published research. As an interim report, it does not present findings on the effects of the programs on student outcomes. Future reports from the randomized controlled trial, which started in summer 2013, will describe the effects of these programs on students' academic and social-emotional outcomes. In the meantime, however, in response to the growing demand for guidance in this field, we present what we have learned so far about managing summer learning programs. Because we are not able to include evidence of the effectiveness of summer programs in improving student achievement, the practices we recommend in this report should be considered promising, but not proven.

Highlights from Research on Summer Learning

A body of research has documented that summer learning programs can be effective in improving student achievement and providing enrichment activities such as sports, arts, and science exploration for low-income students. Studies have also identified the features of summer learning programs that are associated with improved student performance, results that helped us focus our data collection efforts for the district evaluations in summer 2011. We summarized that research in our earlier report, *Making Summer Count* (McCombs et al., 2011), and give a brief recap of the literature here.

Positive effects on student achievement have been documented for small, voluntary summer programs not run by districts (Borman, Benson, and Overman, 2005; Schacter and Jo, 2005; Chaplin and Capizzano, 2006; and Borman, Goetz, and Dowling, 2009), district-run mandatory summer programs (Jacob and Lefgren, 2004; Matsudaira, 2008; and McCombs, Kirby, and Mariano, 2009), and nonclassroom-based, reading-at-home programs (Kim, 2006; Kim and White, 2008; and Allington et al., 2010). The combined evidence from these studies suggests that all of these types of summer learning programs can reduce summer learning losses and even lead to achievement gains. Moreover, some longitudinal studies conclude that the effects of a summer learning program can endure for at least two years after the student's participation (Jacob and Lefgren, 2004; Matsudaira, 2008; and McCombs, Kirby, and Mariano, 2009).

Besides stemming summer learning loss, summer learning programs can also help bridge the opportunity gap between disadvantaged and advantaged students. Parents with lower incomes are unable to make as many investments in their children's enrichment experiences, so students at the lowest income levels are far less likely than more-affluent peers to participate in lessons, athletics, or clubs, and they are less likely to have access to computers (Kaushal, Magnuson, and Waldfogel, 2011). In addition, many schools and districts, particularly high-poverty and/or lower-achieving schools and districts, have cut school-day enrichment, such as music and art, either to reduce budgets or to maximize time dedicated to core academic content areas (McMurrer, 2007). In 2000, the data showed that 100 percent of high-poverty schools offered music instruction, but as of 2011, only 80 percent offered music instruction. The percentage of these schools offering visual arts, dance, and theater is even lower (Parsad and Spiegelman, 2012).

While the research is clear that summer learning programs can benefit students, not all summer learning programs studied have resulted in positive outcomes for enrollees (Kim, 2004; Borman, Goetz, and Dowling, 2009; and Kim and Guryan, 2010). Research studies and best-practice literature show that effective programs providing high-quality academic opportunities share a number of features:

- **structured instruction** in reading, writing, and mathematics. Instruction should be consistent with state and local content standards and match students' academic needs.
- **adequate intensity and duration of instruction**. Experts recommend that academic instruction last at least three hours a day, five days a week, for five to six weeks.
- **certified teachers** providing academic instruction. Academic instructors should hold the appropriate certification and be selected because of their interest in and appropriateness for summer instruction of low-achieving students.
- **lower student-to-adult ratios** than those in the regular school year. Lower ratios permit more attention to the needs of individual students.
- **enrichment activities** to supplement academic content. Enrichment activities often involve music, art, sports, and community service and may entail reading and writing. They might be led by regular academic teachers, private program staff, outside contractors, or volunteers from the community. Enrichment activities attract students to attend voluntary programs regularly, incorporate additional hours to a day to make the program more convenient for working families, and help bridge the "opportunity gap" that exists between low-income and

higher-income students during the summer. In some districts, programs try to integrate academic content into enrichment activities.

- **consistent daily attendance**. In order for students to benefit from the summer program, they must regularly attend.

Overview of Demonstration District Programs

The district programs we studied had several common characteristics:

- They offered reading, mathematics, and enrichment activities.
- They operated for a full day.
- They provided transportation to students.
- They were free of charge.
- They served students rising from third into fourth grade during the summer 2011—the only cohort we focus on in the evaluation—but most programs served other grade levels as well.
- The majority of students attending the programs were doing so voluntarily—in only one district were some students required to attend the program due to failing grades.
- They were relatively new. The summer of 2011 was either the second or third year of operation for most of the programs. In two of the districts, Duval and Rochester, summer 2011 was the first year they had operated a full-day program that included enrichment.

While all the districts hosted these programs with the primary goal of improving student achievement, they varied somewhat in their reasons for doing so. The differences reflected the local conditions and priorities within the districts.

- **Duval** and **Cincinnati** used summer learning as part of a school improvement strategy and offered their summer program to all students in the district's lowest-performing elementary schools, which were also schools with very high proportions of students receiving free and reduced-price lunch.
- **Dallas** and **Rochester** arranged their programs to be academic interventions for all low-achieving students throughout the district, many of whom were at risk of grade retention. Through a partnership with Big Thought, an arts intermediary, Dallas incorporated the arts with core academic instruction as a strategy for improving student achievement.
- **Boston** targeted students in certain elementary schools aligned with community-based partners and, in addition to improving student achievement, aimed to improve social and emotional outcomes and build stronger relationships between community-based partners and schools.

- **Pittsburgh** opened the program to all students in the district and strived to create a camp-like atmosphere that aimed to provide urban students with opportunities similar to those available to higher-income suburban students.

Table 1.1 provides more detail about the programs and their differences. As it shows, some districts operated in partnership with local intermediaries, while others were under sole district control. Most districts operated in many sites that served students from different schools, while one district had students attending only their home school's summer program.

All the districts wanted to serve low-performing students, but some districts had more students scoring below proficiency than others. The proportion of students below proficient in either mathematics or English language arts (ELA), as measured on state standardized tests, ranged from 23 to 87 percent across the districts. The districts that opened enrollment to a broader set of students naturally had a large proportion of proficient students, while the districts that concentrated on serving the most-struggling students had the largest proportion of students who scored below proficient in ELA or math on state assessments.

Table 1.1
Characteristics of the Six Districts' Voluntary Summer Learning Programs for Elementary Students, 2011

Characteristic	Boston	Cincinnati	Dallas	Duval	Pittsburgh	Rochester
Number of summers the program operated prior to 2011	1	2	2	2[a]	2	2[a]
Eligibility	Rising fourth-grade students in 13 schools	Students in 16 low-performing schools	Bilingual, 21st Century, and students at risk of grade retention	Students in 21 low-performing schools (excluding lowest-level readers)	All students	All low-performing students
Eligible rising fourth graders	755	809	13,000	1,377	2,130	1,964
Number of rising fourth graders who attended for at least one day	301	160	1,399	224	579	557
Number of summer sites	8	16	17	6	8	3
Leadership structure	District-intermediary partnership	District	District-intermediary partnership	District	District	District

[a] In Duval and Rochester, 2011 was the first year the program operated for a full day.

Approach to Evaluation

Our evaluations focused on the following aspects of the district summer programs:

- planning, management, and quality control processes
- selection and training of instructors
- curriculum and instruction
- enrichment activities
- recruitment and attendance
- time on task
- program cost and funding.

To evaluate these program features, we drew on five sources of information:

- **Interviews.** We conducted 325 interviews with district leaders, program leaders (including external community partners in two of the six districts), school/site leaders, curriculum coaches, academic teachers, enrichment teachers, leaders of the organizations providing enrichment, and teacher aides.
- **Surveys.** Across the six districts, we surveyed four stakeholder groups, as shown in Table 1.2. In this document, we primarily rely on our academic and enrichment teacher interviews when forming our recommendations. For more detail, see Appendix A.
- **Observations.** In five of the six districts, we conducted multiple observations at each site, as shown in Table 1.3. We observed preprogram orientation meetings, trainings, and professional development as well as academic instruction and enrichment programming. Academic observations ranged from 45 to 90 minutes. Observers used an instrument that tracked aspects of the classroom that research indicates are associated with improvements in student achievement, such as productive time on task and individualized attention. Although we used a published protocol for observing the enrichment experiences, we developed our own protocol for observing the academic blocks. After studying published academic

Table 1.2
Total Number of Surveys Across Districts by Respondent

Stakeholders	Number Surveyed	Number Responded	Response Rate (%)
Students	641	641	N/A
Parents	2,209	884	40
Academic teachers	278	186	67
Enrichment teachers	230	148	64

NOTE: We only surveyed students whose parents had given active parental consent and who attended the program on the survey day. In one district, only academic teachers and parents were surveyed (we began our evaluation activities too late to field the student survey).

Table 1.3
Number of Academic and Enrichment Observations Across Districts

Observations	Total
ELA or writing	86
Mathematics	69
Other academics (science and social studies)	17
Enrichment	151

observation protocols, we concluded that we should design our own instrument. The published academic observation protocols focus primarily on rating the quality of teaching. We learned through interviewing the authors of these protocols that establishing inter-rater reliability on these instruments would entail more resources than were available to us. Moreover, we wanted to keep a running time log of instructional activities to capture time-on-task—something that is not captured well in existing observation protocols. Our instrument therefore ensures that observers capture extensive descriptive detail on what is happening in the classroom, without relying on rating scales to measure the quality of the instruction. For more detail, see Appendix A.

- **Curriculum review.** We asked a reading and a mathematics elementary education professor outside RAND to examine the quality of the written ELA and mathematics curricula used in all of the districts except for one, where teachers developed their own curriculum for the summer. The professors did not examine the curricula in this district because each classroom teacher used a different curriculum.
- **District data.** Most demonstration districts operated multiple programs during the summer, of which the Wallace-funded program was just one. We focused strictly on the programs that Wallace funded. (For details about how we analyzed these data, see Appendix B.) We collected the following types of data on students, costs, and funding sources:
  - **Data on all rising fourth graders** in the district as of summer 2011. These data allowed us to examine who enrolled in the program and who actually attended. For each district, we examined attendance rates by site and by demographic characteristics such as achievement on the state assessments in third grade.
  - **Expenditure data** on major cost ingredients such as district-level expenses for program coordinators or secretaries, curriculum development, curricular coaches, professional development, plus school-level expenses for site managers, teachers, enrichment providers, security guards, administrative staff, benefits, classroom materials, field trips, and food. We also tracked the source of these expenditures by funding type (Title I, general funds, 21st Century Community Learning Center, etc.).

The interview protocols, observation protocols, and survey instruments we used are posted online (http://www.rand.org/pubs/research_reports/RR366.html).

In analyzing these data, we prioritized facilitators of and barriers to (1) consistent student attendance; (2) providing at least three hours each day of academic instruction; and (3) teachers' understanding and use of the curriculum, including using it to individually target instruction. We assume, based on prior research, that students will not benefit from these programs unless they are attending consistently and, when attending, are engaged in academic learning that is targeted to their level.

While this report is based upon our evaluation analyses, it is written to be a guide to practitioners. As such, it focuses on outlining promising practices for developing robust summer learning programs.

Report Organization

We organized the report around the key components of summer learning programs and focused each chapter on the recommendations arising from our evaluations so far. Chapter Two is arguably the most important chapter because it highlights how to conduct the planning process for summer, an activity that is crucial to begin early and get right so that other program elements work effectively. The two chapters after that describe strategies to maximize academic quality, including how to choose a curriculum and differentiate instruction for students of different abilities (Chapter Three), and how to select and train teachers (Chapter Four). Chapter Five highlights enrichment, including partnering strategies, activities, and integration of academic and enrichment. Chapter Six describes ways to maximize attendance, and Chapter Seven discusses methods to ensure enough time on task for students to improve their knowledge and skills. Chapter Eight examines funding strategies and costs, with an eye toward achieving funding sustainability through maximizing the impact of expenditures. Within each chapter we describe promising practices that emerge from our observations.

CHAPTER TWO

Planning

Launching a summer program is akin to launching a new school year—albeit more limited, with less time for both planning and execution. It requires establishing a management structure, including district program responsibilities and oversight and site-level leadership and staffing; hiring and training summer teachers and administrators; developing or choosing a summer curriculum; selecting enrichment activities suitable for the program; recruiting summer students and creating ways to promote consistent attendance; and managing many other details, such as transportation, meals, and supplies. These are daunting tasks that require months of planning while the school year is in full swing.

Some districts in the study launched a brand-new program for their third graders; others augmented existing programs. There were not clear differences in the effectiveness of the planning process based on whether the district was launching a new program or planning a summer program that had run in the past.

In our observations of districts, we witnessed the benefits of good planning and the problems created by poor planning. To determine what planning practices worked well, we relied on self-reports from summer program staff and analyzed our interview and survey data for relationships between planning practices and logistics and time for instruction during the summer program. We found that districts in which the planning process was managed well had fewer logistical problems and more instructional time for students. Based on these observations, we present some recommendations on planning.

Start Planning Early and Be Inclusive

Commit to Having a Summer Program by December

Program leaders who decided on a summer program by December and began planning in January ran a smoother summer program with less disruption to academic instruction. When site leaders were hired in January or February, they were able to participate in district-level planning and to conduct their own site-level planning. Planning at both the district and the summer site levels resulted in a smoother start-up to the program and fewer logistical challenges. When teachers were selected in the winter, they were in place to participate in all trainings leading up to the summer programs. When curriculum selection and pacing guide development began in the winter, teachers had these materials with them during training on the summer curriculum. When enrichment providers were identified in the winter, district boards could approve their contracts with sufficient time to pay them for advanced planning, staff hiring, and material purchases.

In those districts where the commitment to a summer program was made later in the school year, there were too many start-up tasks to achieve in a short period of time. For example, late planning led to late hiring and missing curriculum materials. Some teachers were hired so late that they missed the preprogram training sessions. In one district, academic lesson plans were delivered to teachers on the day they were expected to teach them, causing teacher stress and less effective use of class time. In another district, teachers and site leaders lacked sufficient curriculum materials and supplies throughout the summer program. In this district, teachers needed to revise their lesson plans to accommodate the lack of materials and supplies. Late planning also exacerbated the challenges of transportation route planning, particularly in cases where districts allowed late enrollments, as we discuss later.

Include Both District and Site-Level Staff in the Planning Process

Planning appeared to be most effective when done by both central district staff members and the staff who would lead the summer sites. In the districts using this approach, planning was comprehensive because there was sufficient representation of staff responsible for overseeing the various aspects of the program. In the districts in which planning was led solely by the district, participants did not believe they were brought on early enough for site-based planning. In one district, for example, staff members eventually selected for leading the school sites reported that they and their teams were identified too late for effective program planning. Another district decided not to have administrators at each site, relying on teachers to lead sites. This decision led to a number of problems, including an inability to oversee teachers, greet parents, or to send misbehaving students to the office.

Centralize Some Decisionmaking

When done centrally, actions such as identifying student eligibility for the program, choosing a curriculum, designing pacing guides and lesson plans, selecting and train-ing teachers, arranging transportation, and working with community partners ensured a baseline of quality, as perceived by district leaders, across the summer sites. When site leaders are part of the planning process, they can tailor some decisions and actions to their particular sites once these key decisions have been made centrally.

Deliver Planning Templates to Site Leaders

In one effective approach to planning, central office staff created templates that site leaders then used in tailoring policies and procedures to their particular location. For example, central office staff in one district provided sites with a template for incentives that could be used for encouraging consistent student attendance. Individual site leaders then tailored this template so they could implement the incentive programs they found attractive.

Meet Regularly and Be Comprehensive in Scope

Conduct Regular and Productive Meetings

We found that effective planning included regular meetings that focused on developing policies, procedures, and plans. The program suffered in districts that did not hold regular meetings or did not use the time productively. In one district, participants met regularly but reported a low return on the time invested. They felt that less time should have been spent on trust-building activities and games and more time on key issues, such as daily schedules, attendance-taking procedures, material delivery processes, and transportation logistics. Because they did not spend enough time on these topics before the program launched, they experienced serious difficulties with arrivals and dismissals, which may have affected parents' satisfaction with the program experience.

Include Enrichment in the Planning Process

In some cases, districts conducted regular and ongoing planning but it was not sufficiently comprehensive. In one district, for example, the enrichment component of the program did not get enough attention in the planning process. Teachers were hired to teach enrichment blocks without a full understanding of the goals of the program. Some quit after they had more information about the students they were to serve. Furthermore, the enrichment teachers reported that they lacked information on how to handle students' misbehavior. In this same district, an outside community-based organization (CBO) provided some of the enrichment programming. Insufficient planning for this partnership led to confusion about whom to contact about what issues.

Clearly Delineate Roles

Some summer programs are collaborative efforts between community-based or intermediary organizations and the district. When partners are involved in leading the program, the roles for partners, district, and site-based staff should be identified. For example, at the program level, districts and partners should determine who is responsible for selecting curriculum, recruiting students, recruiting and training academic and enrichment teachers, and providing transportation. Similarly, at the site level, if a district staff member and a CBO staff member are leading a site together, the teachers need to know whom to contact for specific issues. We observed confusion and inefficiencies in sites where these divisions of labor were unclear. For example, in one district in which CBOs and district-employed teachers both provided instruction to students, it was not clear which organization had ultimate responsibility to oversee the quality of instruction and manage the instructors.

Establish Firm Enrollment Deadlines and Keep Electronic Student Records

Holding to a firm deadline for enrollment in the summer program has a number of advantages:

- Teachers learn who their students are before the program starts.
- Students can be equally distributed across classrooms and grouped according to performance, if desired.
- Parents can be notified in advance of transportation routes.

Districts with both enrollment cutoffs and sufficient information technology systems and personnel were able to better predict enrollment, assign students to classrooms, assign teachers to students, and direct students to bus routes.

Some program leaders were directed by district policy to allow students to enter their programs at any point during the summer. Such a policy is aligned to school-year policies that allow eligible students to join their public school at any point in time. Although the genesis of open enrollment for summer programs is understandable, the negative impacts are significant.

In these districts without enrollment cut-off dates, students were allowed to join the summer learning program at any point throughout the summer. This factor not only reduced learning time for students who started late, but made it impossible for districts to predict numbers of participants overall and by site. Without this information, districts faced last-minute staffing challenges to meet desired student-to-adult ratios. In one district, which was off by 43 percent on enrollment projections, teachers reported that they did not launch their curriculum on the first day of the program (or even, in some cases, during the first week of the program) because they expected to be moved to a different classroom as program leaders shuffled teachers and students to create classrooms balanced by size and student demographics. In some cases, this shuffling led to teachers teaching grade levels for which they had not been trained. In this district, one-third of the academic teachers had not received any training on the curriculum for the new grade level they ended up teaching. Further, more than a third of teachers reported that they did not receive a schedule or a roster of students until the first day of the program; in the other districts, 90 to 100 percent of the teachers had received this information before the first day of the program and, in many cases, at least a week before the program began. Only half of the surveyed teachers in this district reported that the program was well organized.

This challenge was exacerbated by insufficient information technology support. In one district, parents sent a hard copy of their registration form to their local school, but no one in the school had time to enter this information into a centralized database. Without accurate projections, program leaders struggled to develop class rosters, hire appropriate numbers of teachers, and assign teachers to students.

With students enrolling at the last minute, it was not possible to establish transportation routes early enough for smooth operation. Not having children's home addresses weeks ahead of time forced sites into establishing routes and notifying parents of bus stop locations sometimes within 24 hours of the program's start. In one case, because district or site managers failed to communicate directly with bus drivers, some buses went to each child's home and others went to bus stops, causing confusion and anxiety for parents. In another district, 41 percent of parents surveyed worried about their child getting to and from the program safely at some point in the summer, and 14 percent of parents worried daily. In this district, the chief complaint among parents who responded to an open-ended question about what they liked least about the summer learning program was transportation. In this same district, a program manager cited busing logistics as his main daily challenge. Site leaders reported in interviews that they spent a majority of their time on busing issues and often felt stressed about children getting to and from the program safely.

CHAPTER THREE

Curriculum and Instruction

In any education setting, teachers' instruction of the curriculum has the greatest influence on student learning (McCaffrey et al., 2003; Rivkin, Hanushek, and Kain, 2000). In the context of summer learning programs, the quality of the curriculum and its instruction is critical to achieving the goal of improved student performance. Each of the districts we studied offered at least three hours of ELA and mathematics instruction a day. We assessed their curricula and its instruction in multiple ways: Two external curriculum reviewers (one for ELA and one for mathematics) reviewed curricula; we also surveyed and interviewed teachers and interviewed curriculum coaches and site leaders on their opinion of the curricula, its fit to students' needs, and teachers' instruction. In each district except for one,[1] we observed one to two math or ELA classes each day throughout the programs' duration. The recommendations we present here are based on our observations and other primary data sources; we do not yet have data on the impact of the curricula and its instruction on students' outcomes.

Anchor the Program in a Commercially Available and Tested Curriculum

According to the external reviewers, the districts in the study with the strongest curricula had selected a commercial program. One of these districts' ELA curriculum is highlighted in the accompanying box, "A Promising Approach for ELA." In most of these districts, staff augmented the purchased curriculum with district-developed lessons and activities. In one of these districts, for example, students worked on a district-developed mathematics "problem of the week" that called upon the skills they had been taught that week, without specifying exactly which skills they needed to use to solve the weekly problem.

Although it is not necessarily the case that a commercially available curriculum is preferable to a program developed by a district, curriculum development is time-intensive and best done by curricular experts. In our observations, curriculum plan-

---

[1] We began our evaluation activities too late in one district to conduct these observations.

A Promising Approach for ELA

Teaching ELA Through National Geographic's Science Inquiry Kits on Forces in Motion and Habitats

This district's program is designed for students who have not demonstrated proficiency on measures aligned to state standards for their grade. The overarching goal of the program is to stem summer learning loss for the students who are struggling the most. In 2011, program leaders purchased National Geographic's Science Inquiry Kits on Forces in Motion and Habitats. These kits comprise an integrated reading, writing, science, and social studies model to teach rising fourth-grade students crucial literacy skills. Students learned science and social studies content while engaging in literacy learning.

The curriculum materials included a detailed pacing guide, teacher's guide, and easy-to-access curriculum materials. The curriculum was well organized and easy to follow. Each day followed a predictable routine that included a mini-lesson, work time, and a close. Most of the lesson descriptions set out clear expectations of what the students would do and the activities they were expected to complete. Typically, a single text anchored an entire day's work, creating coherence within lessons, and students' independent work was aligned with the content of the lesson. Throughout the ELA block, students participated in various "hubs" where they were meeting with the teacher in small reading groups or doing other guided activities.

Many aspects of the curriculum were aligned with research findings from recent literacy studies, which make a strong case for focusing reading comprehension on learning content. Unlike many curricula that teach reading strategies in the absence of content, this district opted to anchor literacy learning in two scientific topics: habitats and forces and motion.

A dedicated notebook offered students an opportunity to write often about their science thinking and emphasize important scientific habits, such as recording observations. Students also had wrap-up writing projects that provided them with the opportunity to create a text that was personal (writing about magnet inventions or about a time when a wild animal entered their lives) but also connected to the science content. In addition, National Geographic provided texts targeted for multiple grade and performance levels to support differentiation of activities in the classroom.

ning added another layer of responsibility that was difficult for program staff to manage. In one district that designed its own curriculum, lesson plans were photocopied for teachers just minutes before the class was to begin. In another district, one teacher ended up "working nights and weekends" to finish the curriculum, and, unfortunately, did so only after the scheduled teacher training on the curriculum. Given these constraints, it is not surprising that the commercial curricula were judged to be of higher quality.

Some program leaders resisted the idea of purchasing a commercial curriculum because they believed that summer programs should be "different" and "more fun" than the school year. However, we did not find that student satisfaction varied by district program, despite differences in the approach to curriculum. For example, in a program with a commercial curriculum that described itself as very "school like," 84 percent of students surveyed thought the summer program was fun. In a different program with a homegrown curriculum and a "camp-like" atmosphere, 86 percent of the surveyed students reported that the program was fun—a nearly identical response. Both programs also had similar attendance rates.

Choose Curricula with Features Associated with Improved Learning

There are several reasons why selecting a curriculum for the summer is challenging, including that there are few summer-specific commercial curricula to choose from. Many districts, therefore, adapt a school-year curriculum for the summer, which entails significant work to ensure that the learning goals align to the summer timeframe and that units are selected appropriately. Even when a summer-specific curriculum is selected, district staff augment it with district-specific learning goals and supplementary activities. Involving district curriculum experts is important in this process to ensure alignment to the school year curriculum and goals.

District curriculum experts can then ensure that summer program curricula are structured around the same principles as school-year curricula. For example, class lessons should build on each other: Students should be expected to apply what they learned in one lesson to subsequent lessons. Both the mathematics and ELA curricula used by some districts were judged weak in this area.

Also, the ELA curriculum should incorporate guided reading time or small group reading, offer students a choice of text, and teach reading strategies based on the assigned readings (Foorman and Torgesen, 2001; Shanahan et al., 2010). Students should also be encouraged to write about the readings (Graham, 2010). The ELA reviewer did not find these features in most of the summer curricula we studied. In some districts, we observed classes in which a majority of the class time was devoted to activities that bore little relevance to the subject of the class. For example, in one district's writing block, students were expected to create greeting cards, decorate an author's chair, brainstorm interview questions (that were to be written down by the teacher), and create posters. In many of these activities, students were expected to write almost nothing.

Standardize the Curriculum Across District Sites

In most of the districts we studied, there was one centrally purchased or developed curriculum that all teachers across the district followed in the summer. These districts had the strongest curricula. Teachers found lesson plans clear and easy to follow and all students throughout the program were exposed to the same amount of instruction, targeted toward the same knowledge and skill development.

In a district that had individual teachers developing their own lessons, not all students experienced the same amount of instructional time or type of instruction across sites. We also observed that some teachers prioritized leadership development skills over mathematics or ELA instruction. Although variation in curriculum and experimentation in instructional delivery can benefit both teachers and students, it is important that teachers have a clear understanding of the standards to which they are expected to teach and the time they are expected to spend on instruction.

Include Strategies for Differentiation in Curriculum Materials

In some of the districts we studied, teachers received materials on how to differentiate their lessons during the school year. In one district, teachers were presented with daily lesson plans, along with activities for students who were struggling and activities for students who needed additional challenges.

Most of the districts, however, did not provide this information for the summer program teachers. This could be because the students targeted for these programs are, for the most part, low-performing students, and curriculum planners may have assumed skill-level homogeneity. But teacher reports provided evidence to the contrary. In some districts, many teachers reported great differences in knowledge and skills across students and that they struggled to ensure their lessons challenged both low- and higher-performing students. Ideally, students would be assessed with curriculum-based pretests and split into at least two different ability groups within the classroom, with instruction differentiated by group (Elbaum et al., 1999; Foorman and Torgesen, 2001; Grouws, 2004).

In two of the districts, students with very low reading skills attended a separate program that developed early literacy skills. In these districts, teachers were more likely to report that they were able to challenge both high- and low-achieving students during the summer. Although separating students into independent programs is not always feasible, or even desirable, teachers should have the curricular resources to target instruction to at least two different ability groups.

Structure for Sufficient Time on Task

All of the districts planned for a certain number of minutes each day to be devoted to mathematics and ELA. Curriculum pacing guides were developed based on this time allocation. Most of the districts struggled to meet these time-on-task goals. Reasons for falling short included site leaders not scheduling classes for a sufficient duration, teachers spending class time on noninstructional tasks, inadequate transition time between classes, and scheduling special assemblies during academic blocks. The district in which we observed the highest time-on-task proportion emphasized academics as the most important component of the program, provided a standardized curriculum in ELA and mathematics, grouped students into classrooms by ability level, and provided all instruction in traditional classrooms rather than in outdoor settings or other places. (For more on this topic, see Chapter Seven.)

Serve Students in Small Classes or Groups

Teachers may find large class sizes challenging, even if they have a second adult in the classroom. In the two districts with the largest class sizes, program leaders employed a second adult in the classroom. Teachers in these two districts reported the greatest difficulty in challenging both low- and high-performing students. We observed that the second adult in these classrooms spent most of the time on administrative tasks, rather than providing students with instructional support. Teacher aides and paraprofessionals need training to effectively co-teach or provide targeted instruction both to individual students and groups; and none of the districts included teacher aides and paraprofessionals in their curriculum training. If teacher aides cannot be provided with the same training on curriculum, we recommend prioritizing smaller class sizes over two adults in the classroom.

Provide Support to Students with Special Needs

Some of the programs served many students who had school-year individualized education programs (IEPs) that did not specify services during the summer months. Multiple stakeholders responded that it was unfair and unwise to not provide the support that students with IEPs need. Students who need special support during the school year will also need it during an academically focused full-day summer program. Teachers and site leaders alike feared that these students were not benefiting as much from the program as they could have been. Program leaders, however, acknowledged that they lacked the funding to provide these students with the services that they received during the school year. Hiring special education teachers and coaches to assist these students during the summer may ensure that students with special needs receive additional support.

CHAPTER FOUR
Teacher Selection and Training

Research confirms that teacher quality has the largest school-based impact on student outcomes (Sanders and Rivers, 1996; Wright, Horn, and Sanders, 1997; Sanders and Horn, 1998; Rowan, Correnti, and Miller, 2002; Rivkin, Hanushek, and Kain, 2005). In this chapter, we offer early guidance on how to hire effective summer teachers and give them the training they need—critical steps in achieving teacher quality. We base our guidance on both general education research and our first-year evaluations of the summer learning programs, including observations of training and teacher reports about how well prepared they felt for teaching in the summer program.

Recruit and Hire the Right Teachers

Develop Rigorous Selection Processes to Recruit Motivated Teachers

Summer presents an opportunity for struggling students to receive additional time to engage with academic material. To maximize district investments in the summer, districts need to hire their best and most highly motivated teachers.

Some of the districts we studied adopted rigorous selection processes for hiring teachers who were motivated to teach in the summer program. These selection processes included requiring teachers to write an essay explaining their motivation to work in the summer program, conducting interviews with teachers as part of the hiring process, soliciting recommendations from principals, and even observing teachers in the classroom before extending offers. In one district, summer program leaders considered school-year teaching effectiveness measures in the hiring process. Many districts are bound by union regulations, which dictate how teachers are hired for summer, and often these union agreements have bound districts to hire by seniority. In fact, the district that adopted these selective policies had to negotiate with its local teachers' union in order to adopt a new hiring policy for summer. We recommend seeking similar hiring exemptions.

Take School-Year Performance into Consideration

Several districts across the country are developing measures of teacher effectiveness based on student performance, observations of instruction, surveys of students, and other data. Summer program leaders should be able to take these measures into consideration when hiring for their summer programs. One district selected teachers in consultation with principals who would run the summer sites and considered the extent to which teachers had demonstrated significant academic growth for low-performing students as measured by state assessments (see accompanying box, "Performance-Based Hiring"). We found that teachers in this program made good use of instructional time; students had relatively high attendance rates; and students made substantial gains on the pre-post assessment administered by the program leaders to students who were in attendance during test administration days.

Hire Teachers with Grade-Level Experience and, If Possible, Familiarity with the Students

Summer program leaders all recruited teachers from within their own districts. For this reason, all the summer teachers had a college degree and a teaching certificate for

---

Performance-Based Hiring

When initiating the summer program, this district negotiated with the teachers' union to allow a different hiring procedure for the summer program at its lowest-performing schools. The traditional hiring process is limited by two conditions: (1) teachers are not allowed to teach two consecutive years of summer school; and (2) teachers are selected by seniority. The agreement with the union allowed the district to avoid these restrictions and use performance-based hiring for their summer programs. For their lowest-performing schools, many principals reported that they actively recruited their "best" teachers, many of whom had taught in the program in prior summers.

Principals along with district staff, including Human Resources, reviewed all teacher applications in one day. They based their selections on principal recommendations and student performance data from statewide tests. District administrators specifically looked at the amount of growth teachers obtained for their low-performing students. Most of the teachers they selected had taught at the low-performing school site or a feeder school during the school year, experience that made them familiar with the school culture and in some cases even the students they would teach. When discussing the quality of teachers in these sites, principals typically said they had "one or two" teachers who did not perform up to expectations, and "those teachers will not be returning next year."

kindergarten through eighth grade. The elementary certification and college degree suggests that all teachers held the same general mathematical, reading, and pedagogical knowledge. However, research on teacher content knowledge suggests that effective teachers demonstrate deep levels of content and content-specific pedagogical knowledge of instruction and how to teach it (Ball and Bass, 2000; Hill, Rowan, and Ball, 2005; Phelps and Schilling, 2004; Fillmore and Snow, 2002). Summer teachers who have recently taught in either the sending or the receiving grade level are more likely to have deep content and content-specific pedagogical knowledge for the grade of students they are teaching. Some districts assigned teachers to grade levels and subjects that matched the teachers' recent experience—avoiding, for instance, assigning a middle-school physical education teacher to teach third-grade reading. By matching teachers' summer experience to the school-year experience, districts also aimed to maximize teacher knowledge of grade-level standards and children's developmental stages.

Some districts also tried to maximize the number of teachers who had previously taught the students in their class or knew the students from their school. Prior research from a mandatory summer program in Chicago showed that students taught by their school-year teacher during the summer posted larger gains during the summer than other students (Roderick et al., 2003). The researchers theorized that having knowledge of students' strengths and weaknesses enabled teachers to more effectively target instruction.

Give Teachers Sufficient Training and Ongoing Support

Research indicates that teachers need to understand the subject of the training, see it demonstrated, have time to practice it themselves, and then receive ongoing coaching based on their implementation of it (Showers, Joyce, and Bennett, 1987; Joyce and Showers, 2002). Many schools regularly provide this type of support during the school year, and teachers need such support during summer programs as well.

Familiarize Teachers with the Summer Curriculum and How to Teach It

Both the research and our observations confirm that the most important objective of teacher training is to familiarize teachers with the summer curriculum and help instruct them on how to teach it. In the district in which the highest proportion of teachers surveyed reported that they felt well prepared, training consisted of three hours on the ELA and three hours on the mathematics curriculum. We also note that a large proportion of these teachers had previously taught the summer program and used the curriculum in a prior summer, factors that may have contributed to teacher preparation.

Curriculum training needs to focus on practice—how to *implement* the curriculum—and not simply on providing information about the curriculum. Curricular materials often lack specific guidance for teachers. Effective training offers opportunities for teachers and other support staff who will be in the classroom to practice the lessons or activities. In one district, curriculum coaches had teachers work with partners in practicing a lesson. In another district, trainers simply handed out curriculum materials and instructed the teachers to ask questions if they had any.

As one teacher told us:

> It would be more helpful if they could walk us through the curriculum . . . we are supposed to read it at home, but it's the summer! And even if we read the curriculum, we are teachers, we all teach differently . . . if you just give it to us and expect [us] to teach it it's going to get taught in many different ways . . . if they show it to us, then we can get a better sense of what/how they want us to teach.

In this district and others, training on the curriculum, particularly when offered right before the start of the summer program, was often crowded out by discussions of logistics. Teachers came to the training wanting to know how many students they would have in their classrooms, what grade level they would teach, which room they were assigned to, etc. To ensure that sufficient time is spent on training in the curriculum, we recommend that districts address these logistical questions separately. Teachers could be told that they will have all logistical information in hand on a certain date or this information could be provided to teachers prior to the curriculum training. It is likely that if teachers have printouts with scheduling and logistics information in hand, they should be able to better focus on the curricular training.

Help Teachers Tailor the Curriculum for Students with Different Aptitudes

Although most of the curricula implemented in the districts specified that instruction be delivered to students working in ability-differentiated centers or small groups, many teachers struggled to implement this instructional approach and would have benefited from additional training and support. In some districts, we observed more whole-group instruction than was specified in the pacing guides. Moreover, teachers received little guidance on how to differentiate lessons for lower- and higher-achieving students in the training (curricular materials were also lacking in this regard, as discussed in Chapter Three). Teachers struggle to differentiate during the school year, and summer presents additional challenges—the time frame is shorter and the curriculum may not be as familiar. Consequently, training should involve explicit guidance and practice on how to differentiate instruction, and ongoing support for this practice should also be provided.

Provide Ongoing Support to Implement the Curriculum

Instructional leaders, such as coaches, can help teachers implement the curriculum and differentiate instruction. Three of the districts employed curriculum coaches to support teachers during the summer program. They were typically seen as teachers' go-to people for materials, procedures, and support. However, having a coaching position did not ensure instructional support for teachers. In one district, the coaches did not typically support teachers in the classroom. The district with the most successful implementation of coaching during the summer used coaches who worked at the host schools and had existing relationships with the principal of the summer program and many summer teachers. In this case, coaches supported teachers instructionally by observing classrooms, helping to implement small-group instruction, and leading common planning meetings. A district with less successful coaching implementation had every content coach serving more than ten schools. In this case, coaches had difficulty providing ongoing support to any school or teacher. Teachers reported that they would have liked receiving a schedule telling them when adults (coaches and instructional aides) would be "pushing in" to their classrooms so that they could schedule center- or small-group instruction during those times.

Include All Instructional Support Staff in Academic Training Sessions

Some districts provided a second adult in the academic classroom—usually a paraprofessional or, in some cases, a college student. Although this person could have helped differentiate instruction by working with small groups or individual students, we seldom observed such assistance. The additional person was more likely to engage in noninstructional tasks, such as distributing classroom materials, escorting students to the office, or administering a program-developed make-up assessment. Although the lead teachers greatly appreciated this help, we did not find that the additional adult contributed to differentiated instruction or provided individual attention to struggling students. In these districts, these second adults did not participate in the curricular training, which may have contributed to the behavior we observed.

Give Teachers Time to Set Up Their Classrooms

We observed better use of instructional time in the first few days of summer when teachers were scheduled and paid to set up their classrooms before the start of the program. Having time to review materials, learn about the room set-up (including access to technology), test passwords needed for computers and smart boards, and prepare classroom materials such as vocabulary word and other posters reportedly helped ensure that teachers were able to start instructing students on day one of the program. Teachers also indicated that they wanted curricular materials provided to them early, so they could thoroughly review them and ensure all needed materials were on hand before the first day of class.

CHAPTER FIVE

Enrichment Activities

All the districts offered enrichment activities such as the arts, sports, and science exploration, to differentiate their summer program from a traditional "summer school" that
students and parents might perceive as a punitive requirement rather than as a valuable
and fun opportunity. This chapter reviews the goals of enrichment activities expressed
by district leaders and teachers, the different approaches districts took to providing
these activities, and early insights on practices that appear to improve success based
on our classroom observations and teacher surveys. Insights in this chapter are drawn
from our classroom observations of enrichment activities; interviews with site leaders,
academic and enrichment teachers, and support staff; and academic and enrichment
teacher survey data.

Goals and Expectations

Districts had multiple goals and expectations in providing enrichment activities. Those
we heard most often are described here. First, district leaders hoped that by adver-
tising the enrichment activities, they would attract more students than they would
otherwise. They also hoped that students would want to attend regularly once they
became engaged in the activities. In one district, site leaders thought that the addition
of enrichment activities led to improved attendance over prior years. One site leader
in a program that offered drama as an activity said in an interview at the end of the
program:

> Attendance was strong this summer. Typically, attendance has died down after the
> fourth of July, but this did not happen this year, and there is still a lot of excitement
> in the program. The field trips and drama have really helped.

Indeed, creating incentives for students to participate in the program by offering
a range of fun activities has been offered as an effective strategy for maximizing out-of-
school time and summer program participation by practitioners and researchers alike
(McCombs et al., 2011; Lauver, Little, and Weiss, 2004).

Second, districts expected enrichment activities to narrow the "opportunity gap" by providing low-income students some of the cultural opportunities that are typically available to more affluent students during the summer. As one teacher said,

> Kids in poverty are not privy to a lot of experiences during the summer, and we gave them a lot of neat experiences this year. We have an "exposure gap." We are helping to build background knowledge through these field trips and experiences as well.

Another teacher, who was surprised that a substantial proportion of students in the program had never been to a museum that was a major institution in the city, said, "It blew me away to learn students had never been there." Besides museum visits, districts had field trips to annual festivals or theatrical productions, a farm, a public swimming pool, the zoo, the aquarium, botanical gardens, and science centers. One district held assemblies to bring in guest speakers such as career counselors, firefighters, and police officers. In four of the districts, enrichment teachers at each site worked together in planning a culminating activity or production. In districts that held such events, some site leaders felt that the events helped open the school to parents and the community. Enrichment teachers were particularly excited by the culminating events, because many did not have the opportunity to put on productions with students during the school year.

Research confirms that lower-income children are less likely than their higher-income peers to engage in beneficial enrichment activities—such as art or music lessons, vacations, or visits to educational venues like museums, zoos, and libraries (Alexander, Entwisle, and Olson, 2007; Chin and Phillips, 2004; Wimer et al., 2006). These disparities can come into particularly sharp focus during the summer months, when parents are left with the task of finding safe and productive ways for their children to spend their days. While this can be a challenging time for all parents, results from a national survey of parents suggest that low-income and minority parents are consistently less satisfied or more apprehensive about the available options for their child's summer activities (Duffett and Johnson, 2004). Not only is such an "opportunity gap" in enrichment activities important to address in its own right, research suggests that it also contributes to the gap in educational achievement and attainment that persistently falls along income and racial lines.[1]

Third, teachers generally felt that providing enrichment helped a child's personal development, and many mentioned that it was a needed corrective in a school year that crowds out time for these activities. Some emphasized that enrichment activities developed the child's self-confidence, an outcome that should improve academic performance as well. One teacher told us, "This is amazing. I am seeing kids grow in ways

---

[1]   See Miller (2003) for a summary of this evidence.

that on paper are not academic growth. I am seeing them grow as stewards of nature and as investigators."

Finally, some districts used enrichment to reinforce and augment academics. In one district, specific integration classes during the day allowed students to explore academic topics through the arts. Although there were challenges in achieving this reinforcement goal, as we will describe, site leaders believed that some activities, particularly drama, improved academic skills and classroom behavior. One site leader described it this way:

> We see a real benefit in drama. There are kids who came in who were reluctant to speak, and now they are reciting monologues. There is a spillover into the classroom as well. Those students are now responding more to open-ended questions and they are looking adults in the eye. They are building more confidence in their speaking skills.

Research supports these educators' observations. In a review of the literature on after-school programs, Miller (2003) discusses several ways such programs can contribute to personal and academic success. Many of these could be transferable to the enrichment activities provided during a summer program. For example, positive learning experiences through after-school activities—especially when in a school setting—can translate into a more positive identification with school (Gilman, 2001; Marsh, 1992). If enrichment activities are designed to be engaging and fun, students' experiences may carry those positive summer program experiences with them as they start the regular school year in the fall. Similarly, the self-confidence that can be gained when students master a new song or discover a new talent can increase their sense of themselves as capable learners. This shift in self-perception has the potential to influence other aspects of children's lives, including their academics (Jordan, 1999).

Select Providers with Well-Qualified Staff

Districts proceeded quite differently in providing enrichment activities, and we found that all these approaches could work well if well implemented by qualified staff. In some cases, the different approaches reflected the different objectives of the districts and resulted in different types of activities.

Hiring District Teachers

Some summer programs hired certified teachers to provide enrichment activities to students during the summer. These were the districts with summer programs that felt the most "like school" and where district leaders espoused firm academic goals above any others. Enrichment activities provided in these two districts were similar to what schools might offer during the school year—visual art, music, dance, drama, and physical education. One district leader noted that arts instruction, which had been dropped during the normal school year, would help narrow the opportunity gap for students in the summer program.

Contracting Directly with Enrichment Providers

One district issued a request for proposals (RFP) in August, and initial proposals from CBOs were submitted in November. Responding CBOs were required to develop an enrichment curriculum that included the reinforcement of academic skills, a schedule, learning goals for the students, projections of the number of students they could serve, and a budget. Proposals were scored on a rubric and voted on by a selection team. Of 72 submitted proposals, 52 were selected, and eight worked with the rising fourth-grade students. In its attempt to narrow the opportunity gap, this district offered a great variety of programming across multiple grades, which included fencing, swimming, studio art, biking, science, and drama.

Another district contracted out as well, but in a different way. Rather than issuing an RFP, school-based after-school coordinators worked to find CBOs to provide enrichment activities during the summer program. Many of these enrichment providers worked with the schools during the school year. As a result, they were familiar with the school and many of the students. Here, too, enrichment activities were varied, intended to address the opportunity gap, and included step team, hip hop dance, jewelry-making, instruction in etiquette and behavior, sewing, Girl Scouts, disc-jockeying, martial arts, African dance, storytelling and drama, and gardening.

Establishing Strategic Partnerships with Intermediaries

In two cases, a district and an intermediary organization collaborated on developing the summer program. In one district, both district fine arts teachers and local artists hired by that intermediary provided arts-based enrichment, and the program included an explicit arts/academic integration block in addition to a studio arts period.

In the other district, the intermediary brokered partnerships between local CBOs and schools, and each CBO was responsible for its own summer program. Each organization set its own summer schedule, worked with district principals to hire its own academic and enrichment teachers, and was responsible for developing instructional lessons. One of the CBOs, which operated four summer sites, focused on teaching children how to play tennis in the afternoons. At another summer site, students rotated across four activities taught by athletic coaches: basketball, softball, swimming, and double Dutch (a jump-rope game). Three of the CBOs were located in outdoor settings—a nature center, an island, and a nature reservation. Each of these sites provided enrichment activities often using a science-oriented curriculum, in which students explored their natural environment and learned about animals and wildlife while engaging in activities such as hiking, exploring the beach, swimming, archery, and ropes courses.

Plan Carefully If Enrichment Is Integrated with Academics

Not all enrichment activities need to be—or perhaps should be—linked to academic content. But if districts are pursuing this goal, they are more likely to succeed if they conduct careful planning, offer specific curricular guidance and additional training, and promote greater coordination of academic and enrichment staff.

The best examples of the integration of academic content and enrichment we observed were those in which academic content was naturally embedded in the enrichment activity, such as drama (where students were reading and writing), music (where students used fractions to measure rhythms), and nature explorations (where students applied science concepts).

In some cases, however, enrichment teachers reported that they were not provided enough guidance on how to integrate or reinforce academic content successfully and meaningfully into lessons. As a result, both academic and enrichment content suffered. For instance, in one archery lesson, the goal was to have students multiply two-digit numbers by multiplying the number of times students shot an arrow that hit the target, but students hit the target so few times that the class wound up multiplying single digits. In another case, we observed lessons where students were to imitate weather patterns through dance. However, the science of the weather patterns was absent and students did not receive any formal dance instruction.

Another key barrier to successful integration was the separation of academic and enrichment staff. In several districts, academic teachers taught in the morning and then departed in the afternoon when enrichment teachers took over. But even in cases where academic and enrichment teachers were both in the classroom, the two teachers rarely worked meaningfully together. We did not observe team-teaching. Enrichment staff played minimal roles in the academic classes, and academic teachers would act as observers or disciplinarians during enrichment activities.

Hire Instructors Who Can Manage Behavior and Keep Class Sizes Small

The district in which most enrichment teachers had no difficulties with managing classrooms (as confirmed in our observations) hired teachers with experience managing classrooms of elementary students. This district also kept class sizes small—the same size as the academic classes. Smaller class size is considered a best practice in summer learning programs (McCombs et al., 2011) and the literature reinforces this district's experience that smaller class sizes can support more effective behavior management by increasing student engagement and decreasing disruptive student behavior.[2] As a result, only about one-quarter of enrichment teachers reported that class size prevented

---

[2]   See Finn, Pannozzo, and Achilles (2003) for a review of this literature.

them from individualizing instruction and that student misbehavior resulted in wasted instructional time, compared to half to three-quarters of enrichment teachers in other districts.

In other districts, classes of students were combined during enrichment periods, resulting in larger class sizes. But enrichment teachers and their assistants did not always have experience instructing large groups of students. The enrichment teaching force in districts that partnered with CBOs ranged from experienced professionals (e.g., studio artists) to college and high-school students. In addition, many enrichment instructors did not receive behavior management training. In these districts, we observed difficulties with disruptive students, and the teachers reported that such disruption resulted in wasted instructional time. One enrichment teacher said, "Too many kids whose behavior was off were pulling the energy from the majority who were here to learn."

CHAPTER SIX

Attendance

The ultimate goal of the districts' summer programs is to improve student achievement. Offering a high-quality program is only part of this task: Districts also need to attract students to the program and ensure consistent attendance. Studies that have examined the link between outcomes and attendance have found that increased attendance is correlated with academic outcomes (McCombs, Kirby, and Mariano, 2009; Borman and Dowling, 2006). None of the district programs were funded based on attendance. Nonetheless, all program leaders hoped to maximize student participation. Because most of the districts knew it would be a challenge to get students to attend voluntary summer programs on a regular basis, they developed strategies to maximize attendance rates. Some of these were more successful than others. In this chapter, we describe the practices that appeared to be most effective in attracting and keeping students, based on observations and interviews with site leaders, academic and enrichment teachers, along with an analysis of attendance data in each district.

Set Enrollment Deadlines

While there is an understandable desire to serve all students who need the program regardless of when they sign up, there are high costs to a rolling enrollment policy and distinct benefits to setting enrollment deadlines. We have already pointed out that enrollment deadlines are necessary for program planning: When districts can predict enrollment, they can also assign students to classrooms, assign teachers to students, and plan bus routes. But setting enrollment cut-off dates is important for other reasons as well: It ensures higher average daily attendance rates and it improves learning. If a student enrolls halfway through the program, it would be impossible for that student to have an average daily attendance rate of more than 50 percent, with implications for learning. Moreover, some interviewees suggested that open enrollment conveyed the wrong message to parents. One interviewee lamented:

> [There are] camps that students go to for a week, and then [they] come back. The district feels that anyone can enroll at any time; so it's hard to say, "You can't miss any days." The district sets a culture for not caring if students come all X days.

Establish a Clear Attendance Policy and Track Attendance

Setting clear expectations appears to be an effective strategy for achieving strong attendance. The program with the strongest attendance had a large proportion of students who had been told summer program attendance was required to meet grade promotion. Clearly, tying summer programming to grade promotion is a strong attendance incentive. Studies of other mandatory programs (Roderick et al., 2003; McCombs, Kirby, and Mariano, 2009) report strong attendance rates in these programs.

While voluntary programs do not carry the "stick" of retention to encourage participation, some of these programs set attendance expectations and policies to encourage regular attendance. For instance, students who missed more than three days of one district's summer program could be removed from the program. Almost all academic teachers in this district (97 percent) reported that site administrators made attendance expectations clear to parents, higher than the proportion found in other districts. Site leaders followed up on these expectations by phoning parents when students were absent to inquire about the reason for the absence and to encourage continued attendance. Districts that reinforced the need for consistent attendance in application materials typically had better attendance rates than summer programs with loose, unarticulated attendance policies.

Provide Field Trips and Other Incentives for Students Who Attend

Field trips and other rewards for participation appeared to improve attendance rates. For example, several districts required that students attend a certain number of days during the week of the field trip to be allowed to join the trip. Some districts also used small incentives such as public recognition, treats, games, and parties as rewards for strong attendance. The district with the lowest average daily attendance rate did not provide student incentives to encourage attendance.

Student incentives appear to be more powerful when combined with attendance expectations and an enrollment cutoff, a finding corroborated by other programs' experiences (McCombs et al., 2011). Student incentives alone are not a panacea. The two districts that worked the hardest to incentivize students had very different attendance rates. In one, which had an 83 percent average daily attendance rate, incentives were paired with an explicit attendance policy. Another district, which had a 66 percent average daily attendance rate, offered a number of ongoing incentives to students but did not have an attendance policy or enrollment cutoff date.

Because parents of elementary school children influence their children's attendance, one district asked RAND researchers to test the impact of parent incentives on attendance. All elementary students' parents were randomly assigned either to receive an incentive for attendance or to serve in a control group. Parents of "treated" children received a $50 grocery/gas gift card if their child attended eight of ten days in the first two weeks of the program and then they received a second grocery gift card of higher value ($70) if their child attended ten of the 13 days in the second half of the program. Parents of "control" children received nothing for attendance. The parent incentive resulted in marginal but statistically significant effects. However, the positive effects from the incentives appeared to be concentrated at the upper end of the attendance distribution—that is, students who were already attending at high rates were the ones responding to the incentives (Martorell et al., 2012). Despite the positive effects of the parent incentives, the benefits do not appear to exceed the costs. The program still suffered from low overall average daily attendance rates (less than 70 percent), despite the prevalence of attendance incentives, a somewhat puzzling finding. In addition, the incentives did not boost the attendance rates of poor attenders.

Disguising Academics Is Not Necessary to Boost Attendance

In the summer learning field, program designers debate whether camp-like programs that "mask" learning have stronger attendance than more traditional programs that have explicit academic objectives. Our examination does not find a relationship between the type of program and attendance. Among the six districts, the two strictly

---

Combining Strategies to Maximize Attendance

One district, with a six-week, academically focused program, set an attendance policy that was clear in all its promotional materials for the program: Students were not to miss more than three days because they needed to attend to benefit from the program. In addition, for the first time, the district established incentives for students to encourage attendance. According to site leaders, teachers, and enrichment staff, incentives combined with field trips worked to keep attendance high. Site leaders reported that dips in attendance after the Fourth of July in prior years were minor this year. Each site designed its own student incentive scheme that included weekly events such as ice cream treats, pizza parties, dance parties, and candy rewards. One site held a water day with water slides and a dunking booth. Depending on the site, these rewards were given for attendance, behavior, and/or performance. At one school, administrators used public recognition as a reward by making announcements over the loud speaker of "positive referrals"—students who had been caught having good classroom behavior, achievement, etc. Site leadership thought this public recognition had motivated behavior as well. The majority of interviewees thought that field trips also improved student attendance.

voluntary programs with the strongest attendance rates had very different programs from one another. One focused heavily on enrichment experiences and worked to strengthen students' social and emotional well-being in addition to improving academic achievement. This program tried to be the least "like school" of any of the summer learning programs studied. The second program with strong attendance was the most like "regular school," and devoted the most hours to academics and the least hours to enrichment. In these cases, the focus of the program did not seem related to student attendance. What they had in common was that both programs offered a high-quality, engaging program that students enjoyed.

CHAPTER SEVEN

Academic Time on Task

Offering a program does not guarantee results. Productive academic learning time is more predictive of student achievement than student time in the classroom (Harnischfeger and Wiley, 1976; Lomax and Cooley, 1979; Fisher et al., 1980; Karweit and Slavin, 1982; Hawley et al., 1984; Karweit, 1985). In other words, how programs use time is critical. Summer programs that last the same number of days can provide very different levels of average time on task depending on average daily attendance, the number of minutes assigned to academics each day, and how instructional time within academic blocks is used—in other words, how much time is dedicated to instruction.

We found a great range in the academic time on task provided to an average student in these programs—from an estimated 37 hours to 121 hours. We calculated this average using the following formula, based on the districts' schedules and on our observations of classrooms:

$$\frac{(\text{Scheduled days} \times \text{average daily attendance} \times \text{minutes of scheduled academic instruction} \times \text{percent of academic instructional time spent on task})}{60}$$

Table 7.1 shows how factors within the district's control influence this average academic time on task, which is provided in the last row of the table. We offer three examples organized from highest academic time on task (#1) to lowest (#3).

Example 1 was the most academically intense in terms of the number of days of programming (30) and the amount of time during the day dedicated to academic instruction (310 minutes). In addition, it posted strong average daily attendance rates and, from our observations of academic instruction, we found good use of instructional time—only 9 percent of academic time was spent on noninstructional activities.

Example 2 has more minutes of daily academic instruction than in other districts and very high attendance rates, but it was the shortest program studied—only 16 days—which lowered the average academic time on task provided to students.

Example 3 has the lowest time on task due to reduced time dedicated to daily academic instruction, low average daily attendance rates (66 percent), and higher rates of noninstruction during the academic blocks.

Table 7.1
Breakdown of Academic Time on Task for Three Districts

Factors Influencing Academic Time on Task	Example 1	Example 2	Example 3
Scheduled days	30	16	23
Minutes of daily scheduled academic instruction[a]	310	240	180
Average daily attendance rate	82% (or 25 days)	93% (or 15 days)	66% (or 15 days)
Percentage of scheduled instructional time actually spent on academics	91%	85%	83%
Average hours of academic instructional time per student per summer	121	51	37

[a] Because minutes of academic instruction varied by site in many districts, we present the average minutes of daily academic instruction in the three districts. We included ELA, mathematics, and science in estimates of daily academic instruction.

In the rest of this chapter, we recommend three practices to help maximize academic learning time.

Operate the Program for Five to Six Weeks

District leaders determine the number of days in the program and the number of hours of instruction a day. The number of programming days depends upon a number of factors, including budget and time needed for school-year preparations (e.g., time to close down the prior school year, time to prepare for the next school year, and time to ensure school facilities receive summer maintenance). Expert opinion on the optimal length of a summer program varies (McCombs et al., 2011); however, it appears a minimum of five weeks may be a good and realistic guideline for districts to follow if desiring to maximize academic time on task. Five to six weeks of programming allows a few weeks for the wind-down and preparatory activities related to the regular school year while still giving students sufficient time on task in the summer programs. Examples 1 and 2 in Table 7.1 clearly show the difference that two additional weeks of instruction make on the amount of academic instruction that students receive during the summer. If a goal of the summer program is to improve academic outcomes, maximizing academic time on task is critical.

Schedule Three to Four Hours a Day for Academics

Three to four hours of academic instruction per day is typically recommended as a minimum.

Not surprisingly, teachers in programs with greater hours for academic instruction were more likely to agree that the program could significantly improve students' academic achievement. We found a great range across districts in time per day scheduled for academics: from 180 minutes to 310 minutes. In the district with the fewest hours scheduled for academic instruction, only 42 percent of teachers reported that the program could make a significant difference in student achievement, compared with 92 percent of teachers in the program with the greatest number of hours scheduled for academic instruction.

Focus on Academic Content During Academic Class Periods

Scheduling time for academic instruction does not guarantee that the time will be used for instruction. Districts varied by 10 percentage points (from 81 to 91 percent) in the time spent on academic instruction during the academic segments of the program. A few practices appear to be related to effective use of classroom time: Adopting a clear, effective curriculum with an expectation that teachers follow it; scheduling time for students to move from one class to another; hiring strong teachers; and clearly articulating that academic achievement is an important goal of the program.

CHAPTER EIGHT

Program Cost and Funding

Cost is of utmost concern to school districts in deciding whether and how widely to offer summer programming. In this chapter we describe the amount of "new money" districts required to operate a summer program—that is, the direct monetary expenditures in the districts' 2011 summer budgets, not including such "hidden costs" as the use of school facilities at no charge to summer program budgets or the in-kind provision of district administrator time for planning or carrying out the summer program. Based on cost data we collected from six school districts, we describe the sources of this funding, distribution of costs, the average costs per student served, and the factors that influenced those costs. In the end, we recommend ways that districts can control costs while designing a program that meets students' needs. (For a fuller description of our cost analysis, see Appendix B.)

Sources of Funding

Districts relied on many sources of funding, as shown in Figure 8.1. Title I funds were the most common funding source, averaging slightly more than half of all revenues. Approximately 80 percent of district revenues came from federal or local school district funding sources, such as Title I, 21st Century Community Learning Center (21CCLC) funds, School Improvement Grants (SIG) dollars, or general-purpose funds.

Funding varied by program component:

- To pay for academic teachers, districts drew on Title I, general funds, or Individuals with Disabilities Education Act, Part B (IDEA-B) for special education.
- To pay for enrichment, districts tended to rely on 21CCLC funds, city funds, or federal stimulus funds.
- To pay for bus transportation, districts often used Title I dollars.
- The cost of federally subsidized meals was passed through the districts since districts were reimbursed at cost through the U.S. Department of Agriculture.

Figure 8.1
Average Revenues by Source, Summer 2011

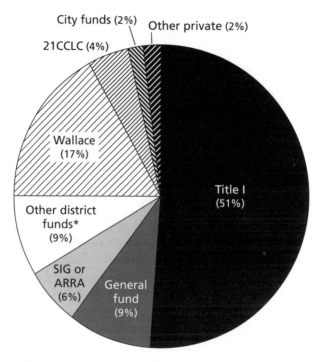

*The "Other district funds" segment consists of Title II, IDEA-B, transportation, and federal meals.
NOTE: The averages shown are based on six school districts' stated revenue sources.
ARRA = American Recovery and Reinvestment Act of 2009.
RAND RR366-8.1

Among private funding sources, The Wallace Foundation was the largest, providing an average of 17 percent of summer school revenues. Other private funds, such as support from local foundations, amounted to only 2 percent of total revenues.

Distribution of Costs

Figure 8.2 shows the average proportion of total costs by category.[1] As anticipated, summer programs spent the greatest share of their funds on academic teachers (45 percent of total expenditures on average); followed by other school-based staff paid for by the summer budget, which included site managers, paraprofessionals, secretarial staff, and nonprofit employees who taught arts, sports, or other enrichment (23 percent on average). District-level costs paid for by the summer budget comprised 10 percent of

---

[1]   Only four out of six districts could provide complete data by category to contribute to this breakdown. Appendix B provides a detailed accounting of reasons data were not available.

Figure 8.2
Average Expenditures by Category, Summer 2011

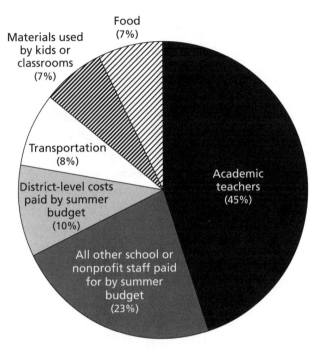

NOTE: Average expenditures shown are based on four out of six school districts' expenditures.
RAND *RR366-8.2*

expenditures on average. (Although districts often contributed staff "in kind" to help carry out summer programs, only those staff directly paid from the summer program budget were included here since districts were not able to systematically account for their in-kind staff contributions.) Busing, materials, and food made up approximately equal shares of the balance of the summer school budget.

Costs and Their Variation

The costs for summer 2011 programs varied widely across districts, which is consistent with findings from previous studies (Grossman et al., 2009; McCombs et al., 2011). They ranged from $8 to $19 per slot per hour (total cost per hour divided by the average number of students present per day) or $7 to $13 per enrollee per hour (total cost per hour divided by the total number of students who attended the program for at least one day).[2]

---

[2]   We calculated these costs using data from five districts. One district did not collect sufficient cost data to be included in our analysis.

Because school districts typically must follow teacher pay scales for summer school programs, teacher wages are often a predetermined component of the overall budget. However, districts can exercise influence over a number of other features of summer programming that have large cost implications. We identified six of these features in our district data:

1. **Attendance rate.** Attendance had a profound impact on costs, inflating program costs by as much as 60 percent more per hour per child in districts with low attendance rates of 63–68 percent. Because districts designed their summer programs to serve a set number of intended enrollees and hired staff accordingly, the costs of the program per slot (i.e., per student served on a typical day) were much higher when attendance was low. Some, but not all, of the voluntary summer programs struggled to maintain strong attendance.

2. **Size of program.** Generally speaking, the larger programs had lower costs per slot. Based on our direct observations of districts' summer programs, we hypothesize that these efficiencies were derived from spreading the fixed costs of running a summer program—such as curriculum development, planning, professional development, and the formation of partnerships with CBOs—over a greater number of students.

3. **Number of students per summer site within a district.** Over and above the size of the summer program itself, clustering more students per site (i.e., at a school where the program is operated) reduced the cost per slot relative to spreading students over more sites. In other words, some of the fixed costs in summer programming accrue at the building level as well as the district level. In larger sites, some of the fixed costs (such as the cost of a school building principal) are spread over a greater number of students.

4. **Duration of program.** Among the four- to six-week summer programs across the districts, we observed lower costs per slot per hour for longer programs, suggesting there are declining marginal costs from adding hours to the summer program. As is the case for several of these cost-related factors, these savings could derive from the division of fixed costs associated with the summer program over a greater number of hours.

5. **Ratios of children to adults.** Although we lack data on the number of adults per enrollee in all of the grade levels across the six districts' summer programs served, our direct observations of sampled rising fourth-grade classes yielded average ratios of children to adults ranging from 6.5 to 11.6.[3] Assuming these ratios hold for all grade levels within a district's summer program, we find (as expected) that costs per slot hour are higher for programs with fewer students per adult.

---

[3] Although we only observed about 60 percent of the instructional periods in each district, we have no reason to believe that these periods, selected randomly, would over- or underinflate the student-to-adult ratios.

6. **Start-up costs.** New summer programs often require acquisition of new materials and development of policies and procedures that older programs do not.

Understanding these factors can help districts design programs to minimize costs while trying to provide the greatest benefits to students. But it is important to recognize that cost efficiencies can threaten quality. For example, devoting fewer hours to academic instruction can lower costs, but it may also reduce the potential for academic benefits from the program. Larger class sizes (after factoring in attendance) can also reduce costs, but larger classes inhibit individualization of instruction.

In the next section we recommend steps that districts can take to control costs while preserving benefits to students.

Recommendations

Design the Summer Program with Costs in Mind
Avoid Assigning Small Numbers of Students to Many Summer Sites Within a District

While there are benefits to having a diversity of sites participate in the summer program, more sites require more transportation and food delivery, and they often require more school administrators—all of which drive up costs. Each building that students attend requires the presence of at least one supervisory staff to ensure student safety. The cost for supervisory staff, such as a site manager, tends to accrue in nonlinear increments—e.g., one new administrator may be required for every 200 additional students, so that the cost of administration per child at a school with an average of 38 students is substantially higher than cost of administration per child with an average of 186 students.

Use Enrichment Providers to Help Leverage Additional Funds

In one district, enrichment providers funded their own services using their 21CCLC funding. As a result, students were able to engage in fun, interesting enrichment at no additional cost to the district. In two other districts, the fact that the summer program was offering a camp-like experience to low-income students attracted private businesses and local foundations that helped support the program.

Use Enrichment Providers to Increase Duration of the Program

Full-day summer programs typically blend at least a half-day of instruction with a half-day of enrichment activities. These nonacademic activities provide opportunities to hire lower-cost enrichment teachers. However, careful partnering and management are needed to ensure the quality of enrichment programming is high.

Hire Staff to Achieve Desired Ratios Based on Projected Daily Attendance, not the Initial Number of Enrollees

Given the gap between initial enrollment and daily attendance in summer programs, districts could reduce overall spending by anticipating the actual number of students served even as they attempt to reduce no-show rates. But it is wise to have a contingency plan in place, such as a list of teacher applicants interviewed but not initially hired, should the realized student enrollments exceed projections.

Maximize the Value of the Summer Program
Put Resources into Tracking and Boosting Attendance

The cost of programming per student is far higher when attendance is poor. Some costs are relatively fixed, such as planning for professional development and transportation routes, the development or selection of curricula, and the time spent for CBOs and school districts to form partnerships. These costs are similar whether a program serves 50 or 500 students. A large gap between initial enrollment and daily attendance inflates costs on a per-child basis, however.

Operate Full-Day Programs for Five to Six Weeks

On an hourly basis, longer programs tend to have lower costs per child served. They also have greater potential to boost student learning over the summer.

Use Effective Cost Accounting Practices
Express Costs on a Per-Enrollee and Per-Attendee Per-Hour Basis

Designers of summer programs could improve their planning process by collecting costs in such a way that they could generate estimates per enrollee and per attendee per hour. Tracking costs in this manner is more accurate than simply adding together budget allocations and dividing by the intended number of students served—and it would aid designers' ability to integrate cost considerations into their program design.

Set Up Three Data Procedures to Enable Cost-Tracking on a Per-Attendee, Per-Hour Basis

To generate cost estimates on a per-unit basis, districts need to ensure that there are accounting practices in place prior to the beginning of the summer program that would allow them to do the following three activities:

- Identify the major ingredients in a summer program (e.g., number of staff by type, number of administrators by type, materials, field trips, food, busing, facilities, etc.).
- Ensure that expenditure data are collected in such a way that they can be disaggregated by those ingredients.
- Track intended enrollment (upon which staff hiring numbers are presumably based), actual enrollment, average daily attendance, proportion of students who enrolled but never attended, and the hours of programming offered.

CHAPTER NINE

In Conclusion

This report provides recommendations on how to establish and sustain summer learning programs with characteristics that have been associated with student achievement in previous studies. It is our hope that this guide will make it easier for district and site leaders to provide summer programs that offer promise for children who are losing ground to their peers over long summer breaks. Future reports from the randomized controlled trial, which will start in summer 2013, will describe the effects of these programs on student academic and social-emotional outcomes. Because we are not able to include evidence of the effectiveness of these summer programs in improving student achievement, the practices we recommend in this report should be considered promising, but not proven. Nonetheless, this research provides the best information to date on how to get to work on summer learning.

Surveys and Observations

Surveys

We surveyed four stakeholder groups—students, parents, academic teachers, and enrichment instructors—regarding their summer 2011 experience, as described below.

Student Survey. We obtained active consent from parents to survey their children in five districts. (We began our evaluation activities in the sixth district too late to field a student survey.) We administered a pencil-and-paper survey to the students. A researcher read the questions aloud while students followed along and answered questions on the survey form. All students whose parents gave active consent for participation and who were in attendance on the day of survey administration during the last week of the program were surveyed (a total of 641). This number represents 21 percent of the total number of rising fourth graders who enrolled in the five summer learning programs where we conducted the survey. It is likely that we surveyed students who were most satisfied with the program, as attendance in voluntary programs is often considered a proxy for satisfaction.

Parent Survey. We sent surveys to 2,209 parents of rising fourth-grade students attending the six district programs. In five districts, we sent paper surveys home in the backpacks of students during the last week of the summer program, so we did not attempt to survey all parents of rising fourth-grade students. We provided parents with a prepaid business envelope and a promise of a $10 gift card as a token of thanks for their participation. In the sixth location, the district mailed our surveys home to all parents, not just those of students who were still attending at the end of the program. Across the six districts, 40 percent of parents responded (884). Parents were asked about how they heard of the summer learning program; reasons for enrolling their child; satisfaction with aspects of the program such as instruction in English language arts (ELA) and mathematics, enrichment offerings, food, and transportation; any barriers to participation and attendance; and likelihood of enrolling their child next year. We learned quite a bit from these surveys, but because in most districts we only sent the survey home in backpacks, we missed an opportunity to survey parents of students who had dropped out or who attended inconsistently. As a result, the parents surveyed (in five of the six districts) were likely those who were most satisfied with the program.

Academic Teacher Survey. In total, we surveyed all 278 academic teachers of rising fourth-grade students and received responses from 186, for a response rate of 67 percent. In five districts, we administered a paper-and-pencil survey that teachers were to fill out and return to RAND using the provided business-reply envelope; in the sixth district, teachers took an online version of the survey. The survey asked teachers about the quality and pacing of the curricula, student ability, differentiation of instruction, availability of needed materials and supports, professional development, motivation for teaching during the summer, attitudes toward summer programs, methods of engaging students, interactions with parents, use of data, support from site coordinator and district officials, and enablers and challenges to providing high-quality summer instruction.

Enrichment Instructor Survey. We surveyed all 230 regular enrichment teachers (we did not survey guest instructors who only offered one lesson over the summer), also using a paper-and-pencil survey that these teachers were to fill out and return to RAND using the provided business-reply envelope. We received responses from 148 teachers (64 percent response rate). Because the enrichment teachers taught nonacademic subjects, their survey contained fewer items on curriculum and student performance. These teachers were asked about training and experience, availability of needed materials and supports, professional development, methods of engaging students, interactions with parents, support from site coordinators and district officials, and relationships with school personnel.

Observations

We conducted observations of operations, enrichment activities, and academic blocks across sites within five of the six districts. One district was added to the initiative in the last week of their summer program. We conducted some observations in this district, but we did not use the systematic approach, involving rubrics, that we used in the other five districts.

In one of the five districts, we selected a proportion of the school sites to focus on within the total population of school sites. We focused on four of the 17 total school sites because these four sites operated under a partnership between the district and a local CBO. We chose to study these four sites in depth over studying the 17 sites at a more superficial level so we could learn more about sites that were co-led. Co-led sites represented a minority of sites across our six districts.

In the other four districts, we conducted an equal number of observations at each summer school site serving rising fourth graders.

Site Operations Observations

In each of the five districts, we used an operations checklist once a week at each site to monitor schedule compliance, facilities issues, transitions, and unforeseen events.

Academic Observations

We conducted observations of academic instruction in the five districts as well. To create our observation protocol, we first reviewed some widely used validated instruments—such as The Classroom Assessment Scoring System measure developed at the University of Virginia (Teachstone, undated) and The Framework for Teaching developed by Charlotte Danielson and the Danielson Group (undated). These classroom observation instruments, however, were not necessarily designed to analyze aspects of the classroom that research about *summer programming* indicates are the most important features linked to improvements in student achievement. Consequently, RAND developed its own classroom observation protocol to pilot in summer 2011 that was designed specifically to measure certain key aspects of our theoretical framework about how summer programs might lead to gains in student learning.

The classroom observation protocol was intended to gather information on the following practices identified by the research as being related to improved student learning in summer programs.

- **Time on task.** The amount of productive time on task is positively linked to student achievement (Harnischfeger and Wiley, 1976; Lomax and Cooley, 1979; Fisher et al., 1980; Karweit and Slavin, 1982; Hawley et al., 1984; Karweit, 1985). The efficacy of summer programs to improve student learning is a function of the amount of exposure students receive to instruction—in terms of both attendance and real classroom instruction. *How our classroom observation protocol brings data to bear on this topic:* The classroom observation protocol has a running log of minutes spent on instruction versus noninstruction and categorizes the type of instruction occurring throughout the class.

- **Individualized attention.** Individualized attention is linked to achievement gains in summer programs (Cooper et al., 2000). *How our classroom observation protocol brings data to bear on this topic:* Observers recorded each instance of a teacher's extended attention (at least three minutes) to an individual student or small group of students (without noting quality of that interaction).

- **Student engagement.** Student engagement in tasks leads to greater academic achievement (Skinner, Kindermann and Furrer, 2009). *How our classroom observation protocol brings data to bear on this topic:* At ten-minute intervals throughout the sessions, classroom observers counted the number of students who were visually disengaged from the designated classroom activity at that moment.

The protocol also included a basic measure of instructional quality (whether the lesson objective was stated and followed) and a log of minutes according to type of classroom activity, including active participation by students in discussion, students' use of manipulatives, activity hubs, and students' direct engagement with reading connected texts and writing (as opposed to more rote tasks such as worksheets, list making, and filling in blanks).

Enrichment Observations

We used the validated out-of-school time (OST) instrument developed by Policy Studies Associates (PSA) to record observations of enrichment activities.[1] All eight observers who conducted OST observations in the five districts received a daylong training from a PSA researcher on the proper use of this instrument, during which the trainer conducted informal inter-rater reliability tests using videotaped enrichment sessions that each observer rated. Throughout the day, the eight observers watched video clips, completed the OST tool, and then the trainer discussed disparities among the eight observers' ratings to calibrate them. Completing the observation protocol necessitated observing only a 15-minute period of any given enrichment block. During the first week of each district's program, two raters co-observed 15 minutes of enrichment blocks and compared ratings and discussed disparities. After this first week, only one rater observed each studied enrichment block.

Inter-Rater Agreement

We strove to ensure inter-rater agreement on the academic and enrichment instruction observation protocols. All nine observers attended a two-day training on how to use the observation protocols. At this training, observers watched videos of ELA, mathematics, and enrichment classrooms at elementary-grade levels, completed the full observation protocols individually, and then assessed degree of agreement on each item on the observation protocols to calibrate the observers' scoring of the classroom instruction. The group then extensively discussed rating disparities and recoded additional videos to further calibrate rating. Among the observers, four lead RAND researchers then established their own consistency in rating through paired correlations from ratings of further classroom videos. The four lead researchers then participated in co-observations with the RAND staff responsible for field observations. They co-observed ten to 12 classroom segments (each of 15 minutes in duration) in the field during the first week of the summer program in each of the five districts where we conducted classroom observations. The lead researcher and the RAND co-observer collected their ratings on each of 24 items on the observation protocol and their ratings were compared across the ten to 12 classroom segments within each item. Throughout the days of co-observations, the raters discussed disparities to further align their ratings.

---

[1] The OST rubric and documentation for it can be found at PSA's web site (February 2008).

Table A.1 lists the rates of agreement for the academic observations. Note that there are too few co-observations to reject the hypothesis that these levels of agreement could have occurred by chance. Given the low number of co-observations, we do not report Cohen's kappa values.

Table A.1
Rates of Agreement Between Co-Observers

Event Observed	Percentage of Agreement Between Raters
Teacher stated the objective for the lesson	100
The lesson covered the stated objective	100
Total noninstructional minutes spent on student behavior[a]	100
Total noninstructional minutes spent on management (attendance)[a]	91
Total noninstructional minutes spent on "other" activities[a]	82
Total instructional minutes where teacher lectured[a]	91
Total instructional minutes on "initiate-response-evaluate"[a]	82
Total instructional minutes on teacher-led discussion[a]	100
Total minutes of Instruction students working with students[a]	100
Total minutes of Instruction students working silently[a]	91
Total minutes of taking assessments[a]	91
Total minutes of computer use[a]	100
Total minutes of working in activity hubs[a]	100
Total minutes of using manipulatives[a]	100
Total minutes of product-making[a]	100
Total minutes of reading[a]	100
Total minutes of watching videos[a]	100
Total minutes of worksheets[a]	91
Total minutes of writing—complex[a]	100
Total minutes of writing—simple[a]	100
Aggregate number of check marks for behavior-related individualized attention	100
Aggregate number of check marks for academic-related individualized attention from all adults	100
Average number of disengaged students over the recorded observations	72

[a] Raters are deemed to agree when the difference between the number of minutes the two observers of a given code for a given activity was less than or equal to 10 percent of the length of the observed segment (e.g., less than or equal to a one-minute difference for a ten-minute segment).

Cost Analyses Methods and Limitations

Cost Analyses Methods

We used a resource cost model approach (Levin and McEwan, 2001) to estimate the monetary costs of the program based on its ingredient parts. Specifically, we requested districts to report expenditures on major cost ingredients such as district-level expenses for program coordinators or secretaries, curriculum development, curricular coaches, professional development planning, and evaluation; plus school-level expenses such as site managers, teachers, enrichment providers, security guards, administrative staff, benefits, classroom materials, field trips, student bus transportation, and food. In addition to summer 2011 expenditure data, we also sought information about the source of these expenditures by funding type (Title I, general funds, 21CCLC, etc.). Most districts operated multiple programs during the summer, of which the Wallace-funded program was just one. We selected the Wallace-funded program and all grades within that program for this cost and revenue analysis.

Summer programs come in many shapes and sizes. To isolate the source of cost differences to the greatest degree possible, we attempted to hold constant each of the six programs' number of enrollees, attendance rates, program duration, and prices of resources by reporting regionally adjusted costs on a per-slot, per-hour basis. To account for the variation of resource prices across the different cities, we adjusted regionally specific costs into national average costs using the comparable wage index. The costs reported in this section are all specific to summer 2011 and adjusted to national averages unless otherwise noted.

Limitations of Cost Analyses

The intent of these analyses is to represent the amount of "new money" a summer program requires of a school district—i.e., the marginal dollars for summer programming that a district and its partners carried in their summer 2011 budgets. Consequently, we did not attempt to assign value to so-called "hidden costs" such as volunteers,[1] use of school facilities, or the in-kind contribution of staff time for running the program.

We adopted the marginal dollars approach for several reasons. The first is that school districts we spoke with think of total summer program costs in these terms. The second is that in no district were data available to reliably value "hidden costs" or even to account for the amount of in-kind staff hours dedicated to summer programming. However, to the extent that any data *were* available about hidden costs, they indicate that districts heavily subsidize their direct expenditures on summer programming through donated staff time.

Each district encountered bureaucratic barriers that prevented them from easily compiling comprehensive cost data in a way that could be isolated for the summer program in question (rather than lumped together with costs for other district summer programs) and could represent all of the components of the program. The first challenge was that department-based budgeting means that summer program directors often have no idea of the amount of "off-budget" district costs there are for the program—such as for busing, school facilities, food—or for the services of nonprofit partners, such as artists or youth service workers who provide enrichment for the program. A second challenge was the increased effort required to set up accounting procedures ahead of time to ensure that each of the relevant departments or partners track the data in ways that could be aggregated together at the end of the summer program.

In each case where we requested data, a district staff person had to seek out multiple departments to request costs carried in entirely different budgets within the district. For example, the food department's budget includes the cost of federally subsidized meals, the special education department's budget includes the cost of special education teachers to the extent they were present in the summer program, Title I department holds Title I expenses, printing costs are carried within the printing department, and so forth. Once obtained from the respective departments, these costs were not disaggregated by program but combined with other programs such as for all types of summer programming offered. When this specific situation occurred, we estimated costs by prorating the total costs by share of enrollees in all of the summer programs the costs represented. Admittedly, this approach to allocating costs is imprecise, since individual cost items may not be entirely symmetrical across programs (e.g., the amount of printed materials per student may be greater for middle- and high-school students than for elementary students).

In our discussions with districts when collecting costs in this and prior studies, they have reported an exceptionally difficult time accurately determining the cost of the use of their facilities during the summer months for a given program for any one of the following reasons: Many schools are open anyway during the summer for repairs,

---

[1]   We requested information about numbers of volunteers and volunteer hours, but these were unavailable. Our direct observations of the programs during summer 2011 indicated that volunteers were rarely present.

making it hard to isolate the additional facilities costs attributable to a single program; a given school can host multiple programs at the same time; and facilities departments often collect costs in ways that prevent disaggregating them to specific buildings and to specific times of the year. As such, we exclude the cost of facilities even though districts likely did, in fact, incur more costs for using those school facilities than they otherwise would have in the absence of the summer program.

References

Alexander, Karl L., Doris R. Entwisle, and Linda Steffel Olson, "Lasting Consequences of the Summer Learning Gap," *American Sociological Review*, Vol. 72, No. 2, 2007, pp. 167–180.

Allington, Richard L., Anne McGill-Franzen, Gregory Camilli, Lunetta Williams, Jennifer Graff, Jacqueline Zeig, Courtney Zmach, and Rhonda Nowak, "Addressing Summer Reading Setback Among Economically Disadvantaged Elementary Students," *Reading Psychology*, Vol. 31, No. 5, October 2010, pp. 411–427.

Ball, Deborah Loewenberg, and Hyman Bass, "Interweaving Content and Pedagogy in Teaching and Learning to Teach: Knowing and Using Mathematics," in J. Boaler, ed., *Multiple Perspectives on the Teaching and Learning of Mathematics*, Westport, Conn.: Ablex, 2000, pp. 83–104.

Belfield, Clive R., and Henry M. Levin, *The Return on Investment for Improving California's High School Graduation Rate*, University of California, Santa Barbara, Calif.: California Dropout Research Project, August 2007.

Borman, Geoffrey D., James Benson, and Laura T. Overman, "Families, Schools, and Summer Learning," *Elementary School Journal*, Vol. 106, 2005, pp. 131–150.

Borman, Geoffrey D., and N. Maritza Dowling, "Longitudinal Achievement Effects of Multiyear Summer School: Evidence from the Teach Baltimore Randomized Field Trial," *Educational Evaluation and Policy Analysis*, Vol. 28, No. 1, 2006, pp. 25–48.

Borman, Geoffrey, Michael Goetz, and N. Maritza Dowling, "Halting the Summer Achievement Slide: A Randomized Field Trial of the KindergARTen Summer Camp," *Journal of Education for Students Placed at Risk (JESPAR)*, Vol. 14, No. 2, April 2009, pp. 133–147.

Chaplin, Duncan, and Jeffrey Capizzano, *Impacts of a Summer Learning Program: A Random Assignment Study of Building Educated Leaders for Life (BELL)*, Washington, D.C.: Urban Institute, 2006.

Chin, Tiffani, and Meredith Phillips, "Social Reproduction and Child-Rearing Practices: Social Class, Children's Agency and the Summer Activity Gap," *Sociology of Education*, Vol. 77, No. 3, 2004, pp. 185–210.

Cooper, Harris, Kelly Charlton, Jeff C. Valentine, Laura Muhlenbruck, and Geoffrey D. Borman, *Making the Most of Summer School: A Meta-Analytic and Narrative Review*, Vol. 65, Monographs of the Society for Research in Child Development, Malden, Mass.: Blackwell Publishers, 2000.

Cooper, Harris, Barbara Nye, Kelly Charlton, James Lindsay, and Scott Greathouse, "The Effects of Summer Vacation on Achievement Test Scores: A Narrative and Meta-Analytic Review," *Review of Educational Research*, Vol. 66, No. 3, 1996, pp. 227–268.

Danielson Group homepage, undated. As of January 2011:
http://www.danielsongroup.org/

Digest of Education Statistics, "Percentage of High School Dropouts Among Persons 16 Through 24 Years Old (Status Dropout Rate), by Income Level, and Percentage Distribution of Status Dropouts, by Labor Force Status and Educational Attainment: 1970 through 2006," Washington, D.C.: Government Printing Office, 2007, Table 106.

Duffet, Ann, and Jean Johnson, *All Work and No Play? Listening to What Kids and Parents Really Want from Out-Of-School Time*, New York: Public Agenda, 2004. As of March 4, 2013: http://www.publicagenda.org/media/all-work-and-no-play

Elbaum, Batya, Sharon Vaughn, Marie Hughes, and Sally Watson Moody, "Grouping Practices and Reading Outcomes for Students with Disabilities," *Exceptional Children*, Vol. 65, No. 3, 1999, pp. 399–415.

Fillmore, Lily Wong, and Catherine E. Snow, "What Teachers Need to Know About Language," in C. T. Adger, Catherine E. Snow, and D. Christian, eds., *What Teachers Need to Know About Language*, McHenry, Ill.: Delta Systems Co., 2002, pp. 7–54.

Finn, Jeremy D., Gina M. Pannozzo, and Charles M. Achilles, "The 'Why's' of Class Size: Student Behavior in Small Classes, *Review of Educational Research*, Vol. 73, No. 3, 2003, pp. 321–368.

Fisher, Charles W., David C. Berliner, Nikola N. Filby, Richard Marliave, Leonard S. Cahen, and Marilyn M. Dishaw, "Teaching Behaviors, Academic Learning Time, and Student Achievement: An Overview," in Carolyn Denham and Ann Lieberman, eds., *Time to Learn: A Review of the Beginning Teacher Evaluation Study*, Sacramento, Calif.: California State Commission for Teacher Preparation and Licensing, 1980, pp. 7–32.

Foorman, Barbara R., and Joseph Torgesen, "Critical Elements of Classroom and Small-Group Instruction Promote Reading Success in All Children," *Learning Disabilities Research & Practice*, Vol. 16, No. 4, 2001, pp. 203–212.

Gilman, Rich, "The Relationship Between Life Satisfaction, Social Interest and Frequency of Extracurricular Activities Among Adolescent Students," *Journal of Youth and Adolescence*, Vol. 30, No. 6, 2001, pp. 749–768.

Graham, Steve, "Teaching Writing," in Patrick Colm Hogan, ed., *Cambridge Encyclopedia of Language Sciences*, Cambridge, UK: Cambridge University Press, 2010, pp. 848–851.

Grossman, Jean Baldwin, Christianne Lind, Cheryl Hayes, Jennifer McMaken, Andrew Gersick, *The Cost of Quality Out-of-School-Time Programs*, New York: The Wallace Foundation, 2009.

Grouws, Douglas A., "Mathematics (Chapter 7)," in Gordon Cawelti, ed., *Handbook of Research on Improving Student Achievement*, 3rd ed., Arlington, Va.: Educational Research Service, 2004, pp. 162–181.

Harnischfeger, Annegret, and David E. Wiley, "The Teaching-Learning Process in Elementary Schools: A Synoptic View," *Curriculum Inquiry*, Vol. 6, No. 1, 1976, pp. 5–43.

Hawley, Willis D., Susan Rosenholtz, Henry J. Goodstein, and Ted Hasselbring, "Good Schools: What Research Says About Improving Student Achievement," *Peabody Journal of Education*, Vol. 61, No. 4, 1984, pp. iii–178.

Hill, Heather C., Brian Rowan, and Deborah Lowenberg Ball, "Effects of Teachers' Mathematical Knowledge for Teaching on Student Achievement," *American Educational Research Journal*, Vol. 42, No. 2, 2005, pp. 371–406.

Jacob, Brian A., and Lars Lefgren, "Remedial Education and Student Achievement: A Regression-Discontinuity Design," *Review of Economics and Statistics*, Vol. 86, No. 1, 2004, pp. 226–244.

Jordan, Will J., "Black High School Students' Participation in School-Sponsored Sports Activities: Effects of School Engagement and Achievement," *Journal of Negro Education*, Vol. 68, No. 1, 1999, pp. 54–71.

Joyce, Bruce, and Beverly Showers, *Student Achievement Through Staff Development*, 3rd ed., Alexandria, Va.: Association for Supervision and Curriculum Development, 2002.

Karweit, Nancy, "Should We Lengthen the School Year?" *Educational Researcher*, Vol. 14, No. 6, 1985, pp. 9–15.

Karweit, Nancy, and Robert E. Slavin, "Time-on-Task: Issues of Timing, Sampling, and Definition," *Journal of Education Psychology*, Vol. 74, No. 6, 1982, pp. 844–851.

Kaushal, Neeraj, Katherine A. Magnuson, and Jane Waldfogel, "How Is Family Income Related to Investments in Children's Learning?" in Greg J. Duncan and Richard J. Murnane, eds., *Wither Opportunity? Rising Inequality and the Uncertain Life Chances of Low-Income Children*, New York: Russell Sage, 2011.

Kim, James S., "Effects of a Voluntary Summer Reading Intervention on Reading Achievement: Results from a Randomized Field Trial," *Educational Evaluation and Policy Analysis*, Vol. 28, No. 4, 2006, p. 235.

Kim, James S., and Jonathan Guryan, "The Efficacy of a Voluntary Summer Book Reading Intervention for Low-Income Latino Children from Language Minority Families," *Journal of Educational Psychology*, Vol. 102, No. 1, 2010, pp. 20–31.

Kim, James S., and Thomas G. White, "Scaffolding Voluntary Summer Reading for Children in Grades 3 to 5: An Experimental Study," *Scientific Studies of Reading*, Vol. 12, No. 1, 2008, pp. 1–23.

Kim, Jimmy, "Summer Reading and the Ethnic Achievement Gap," *Journal of Education for Students Placed at Risk (JESPAR)*, Vol. 9, No. 2, April 2004, pp. 169–188.

Lauver, Sherri, Priscilla M.D. Little, and Heather B. Weiss, *Moving Beyond the Barriers: Attracting and Sustaining Youth Participation in Out-Of-School Time Programs*, Cambridge, Mass.: Harvard Family Research Project, Issues and Opportunities in Out-of-School Time Evaluation brief series (No. 6), July 2004. As of March 4, 2013: http://www.hfrp.org/out-of-school-time/publications-resources/moving-beyond-the-barriers-attracting-and-sustaining-youth-participation-in-out-of-school-time-programs

Levin, Henry M., and Patrick J. McEwan, *Cost-Effectiveness Analysis: Methods and Applications*, Thousand Oaks, Calif.: Sage Publications, 2001.

Lomax, Richard G., and William W. Cooley, "The Student Achievement-Instructional Time Relationship," paper presented at Annual Meeting of the American Educational Research Association, San Francisco, Calif., April 1979.

Marsh, Herbert W., "Extracurricular Activities: Beneficial Extension of the Traditional Curriculum or Subversion of Academic Goals?" *Journal of Educational Psychology*, Vol. 84, No. 4, 1992, pp. 553–562.

Martorell, Francisco, Trey Miller, Lucrecia Santibanez, Catherine H. Augustine, and Jennifer Sloan McCombs, "Experimental Evidence on the Impact of Incentives for Summer School Attendance," paper presented at AEFP Annual Conference, Boston, Mass., March 15–17, 2012.

Matsudaira, Jordan D., "Mandatory Summer School and Student Achievement," *Journal of Econometrics*, Vol. 142, No. 2, 2008, pp. 829–850.

McCaffrey, Daniel F., Daniel Koretz, J. R. Lockwood, and Laura S. Hamilton, *Evaluating Value-Added Models for Teacher Accountability*, Santa Monica, Calif.: RAND Corporation, MG-158-EDU, 2003. As of March 4, 2013:
http://www.rand.org/pubs/monographs/MG158.html

McCombs, Jennifer Sloan, Catherine H. Augustine, Heather Lee Schwartz, Susan J. Bodilly, Brian McInnis, Dahlia S. Lichter, and Amanda Brown Cross, *Making Summer Count: How Summer Programs Can Boost Children's Learning*, Santa Monica, Calif.: RAND Corporation, MG-1120-WF, 2011. As of June 24, 2013:
http://www.rand.org/pubs/monographs/MG1120.html

McCombs, Jennifer Sloan, Sheila Nataraj Kirby, and Louis T. Mariano, *Ending Social Promotion Without Leaving Children Behind: The Case of New York City*, Santa Monica, Calif.: RAND Corporation, MG-894-NYCDOE, 2009. As of August 24, 2010:
http://www.rand.org/pubs/monographs/MG894.html

McMurrer, Jennifer, *Choices, Changes, and Challenges: Curriculum and Instruction in the NCLB Era*, Washington, D.C.: Center on Education Policy, 2007.

Miller, Beth M., *Critical Hours: Afterschool Programs and Educational Success*, Quincy, Mass.: Nellie Mae Education Foundation, May 2003. As of March 4, 2013:
http://www.nmefoundation.org/getmedia/08b6e87b-69ff-4865-b44e-ad42f2596381/Critical-Hours?ext=.pdf

Parsad, Basmat, and Maura Spiegelman, *Arts Education in Public Elementary and Secondary Schools: 1999–2000 and 2009–10*, Washington, D.C.: National Center for Education Statistics, Institute of Education Sciences, U.S. Department of Education, NCES 2012–014, 2012. As of April 17, 2012:
http://nces.ed.gov/pubsearch/pubsinfo.asp?pubid=2012014rev

Phelps, Geoffrey, and Stephen Schilling, "Developing Measures of Content Knowledge for Teaching Reading," *Elementary School Journal*, Vol. 105, No. 1, 2004, pp. 31–48.

PSA—*See* Policy Studies Associates.

Policy Studies Associates, *OST Observation Instrument and Report on Its Reliability and Validity*, web page, February 2008. As of January 2011:
http://www.policystudies.com/studies/?id=30

Reardon, Sean F., "The Widening Academic Achievement Gap Between the Rich and the Poor: New Evidence and Possible Explanations," in Richard Murnane and Greg J. Duncan, eds., *Whither Opportunity? Rising Inequality and the Uncertain Life Chances of Low-Income Children*, New York: Russell Sage Foundation Press, 2011.

Rivkin, Steven G., Eric A. Hanushek, and John F. Kain, *Teachers, Schools, and Academic Achievement*, Cambridge, Mass.: National Bureau of Economic Research, NBER Working Paper # W6691, 2000.

———, "Teachers, Schools, and Academic Achievement," *Econometrica*, Vol. 73, No. 2, 2005, pp. 417–458.

Roderick, Melissa, Mimi Engel, Jenny Nagaoka, Brian A. Jacob, Sophie Degener, Alex Orfei, Susan Stone, and Jen Bacon, *Ending Social Promotion: Results from Summer Bridge*, Chicago, Ill.: Consortium on Chicago School Research, 2003. As of July 9, 2012:
http://ccsr.uchicago.edu/sites/default/files/publications/p59.pdf

Rowan, Brian, Richard Correnti, and Robert J. Miller, "What Large-Scale Research Tells Us About Teacher Effects on Student Achievement: Insights from the Prospects Study of Elementary Schools," *Teachers College Record*, Vol. 104, No. 8, 2002, pp. 1525–1567.

Sanders, William L., and Sandra P. Horn, "Research Findings from the Tennessee Value-Added Assessment System (TVAAS) Database: Implications for Educational Evaluation and Research," *Journal of Personnel Evaluation in Education*, Vol. 12, No. 3, 1998, pp. 247–256.

Sanders, William L., and June C. Rivers, *Research Progress Report: Cumulative and Residual Effects of Teachers on Future Student Academic Achievement: Tennessee Value-Added Assessment System*, Knoxville, Tenn.: University of Tennessee Value-Added Research and Assessment Center, 1996.

Schacter, John, and Booil Jo, "Learning When School Is Not in Session: A Reading Summer Day-Camp Intervention to Improve the Achievement of Exiting First-Grade Students Who Are Economically Disadvantaged," *Journal of Research in Reading*, Vol. 28, No. 2, 2005, pp. 158–169.

Shanahan, Timothy, Kim Callison, Christine Carriere, Nell K. Duke, P. David Pearson, Christopher Schatschneider, and Joseph Torgesen, *Improving Reading Comprehension in Kindergarten Through Third Grade: A Practice Guide*, NCEE 2010-4038, Washington, D.C.: National Center for Education Evaluation and Regional Assistance, Institute of Education Sciences, U.S. Department of Education, 2010. As of February 20, 2013:
http://ies.ed.gov/ncee/wwc/practiceguide.aspx?sid=14

Showers, Beverly, Bruce Joyce, and Barrie Bennett, "Synthesis of Research on Staff Development: A Framework for Future Study and a State-of-the-Art Analysis," *Educational Leadership*, Vol. 45, No. 3, 1987, pp. 77–87. As of April 10, 2012:
http://www.ascd.org/ASCD/pdf/journals/ed_lead/el_198711_showers.pdf

Skinner, Ellen A., Thomas A. Kindermann, and Carrie J. Furrer, "A Motivational Perspective on Engagement and Disaffection: Conceptualization and Assessment of Children's Behavioral and Emotional Participation in Academic Activities in the Classroom," *Educational and Psychological Measurement*, Vol. 69, No. 3, 2009, pp. 493–525.

Teachstone.org home page, undated. As of January 2011:
http://www.teachstone.org/about-the-class/

U.S. Department of Education, "The Nation's Report Card," homepage, undated. As of April 4, 2012:
http://nationsreportcard.gov

Wimer, Christopher, Suzanne M. Bouffard, Pia Caronongan, Eric Dearing, Sandra Simpkins, Priscilla M.D. Little, and Heather Weiss, *What Are Kids Getting Into These Days? Demographic Differences in Youth Out-Of-School Time Participation*, Cambridge, Mass.: Harvard Family Research Project, 2006. As of March 4, 2013:
http://www.hfrp.org/out-of-school-time/publications-resources/what-are-kids-getting-into-these-days-demographic-differences-in-youth-out-of-school-time-participation

Wright, S. Paul, Sandra P. Horn, and William L. Sanders, "Teacher and Classroom Context Effects on Student Achievement: Implications for Teacher Evaluation," *Journal of Personnel Evaluation in Education*, Vol. 11, 1997, pp. 57–67.